Sun, Yat-sen
The principle of demo-
cracy

| | DATE DUE | |
|---|---|---|
| OCT 20 Ret | OCT 21 2013 | |
| NOV RET | | |
| DEC RET | | |
| | | |
| | | |
| | | |
| | | |
| | | |
| | | |

D1596397

# THE PRINCIPLE OF DEMOCRACY

*By*
### SUN YAT-SEN

*Translated into English by* **Frank W. Price** （畢 範 宇）

*Abridged and edited by the Commission for the Compilation of the History of the Kuomintang*

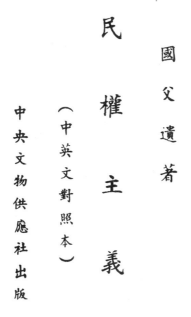

民權主義

（中英文對照本）

國父遺著

中央文物供應社出版

## GREENWOOD PRESS, PUBLISHERS
### WESTPORT, CONNECTICUT

Reprinted from an edition published
by the China Cultural Service, Taipei, Taiwan in 1953

First Greenwood Reprinting 1970

Library of Congress Catalogue Card Number 70-98797

SBN 8371-3147-2

Printed in the United States of America

## PREFACE TO THE ABRIDGED EDITION

Dr. Sun Yat-sen uprooted one of the oldest systems of monarchical rule, which had enjoyed a continuous existence for upward of about four thousand years in China, to establish the first republic in the Far East. Yet he was not merely a great revolutionary leader. He was a great thinker and far-sighted statesman, with clear vision and lofty ideals. In the early part of his revolutionary career, he had already envisaged the irresistible forces of social and economic democracy which must be incorporated in the programme of nationalist revolution in its broader sense. Furthermore, he realized that without a proper adjustment of political rights, social justice and economic equity, any achievement in a nationalist revolution would prove to be fruitless as national stability and prosperity could never be attained. Hence, he was the first leader in China to combine nationalism and political and social democracy into an integral system of political and social philosophy of his own, known as *San Min Chu I*, which provides today the guiding principles for the freedom-loving people of China.

Dr. Sun had the Socratic habit of expounding his system of thought without manuscripts provided beforehand. An eloquent and moving orator, he delivered most of his speeches extemporaneously, interspersed with stories and explanations in popular language to suit the intellectual level and psychological reactions of his audience. The present volume, *San Min Chu I*, was based upon the

i

stenographic notes, often haphazard, of a series of lectures which he delivered before a mixed audience in the auditorium of the Teachers' College, Canton, in 1924. It was his original plan to deliver six lectures on each of his three principles, but he left the last two lectures on the Principle of the People's Livelihood undelivered, because he had to leave the city in order to lead an expedition against the Northern militarists. Recently I am happy to learn that his disciple, President Chiang Kai-shek, is preparing to make the finishing touches for the third part of this work in the form of two additional chapters.

Because of the extemporaneous origin of these lectures, Dr. Frank W. Price, the translator of this book, stated that he had encountered many difficulties in preparing the English translation, as "the constant repetition for the sake of emphasis and the looseness of Chinese *Pai-hua* (spoken language) construction make the original quite a lengthy book." The present abridged edition, prepared by Prof. Wen-yen Tsao, J.S.D., in comformity with an abridged Chinese text recently published in Taiwan, renders a useful and valuable service to readers who are interested in promoting "a better understanding abroad of the great forces that are now driving China forward."

Since the time when Dr. Sun delivered those lectures, the political, military and economic situation, both national and international, has greatly changed. Some of the passages that suited the circumstances and temperament of that period may at present retain only a historical value. With this historical perspective in mind, one can have a deeper understanding and better appreciation of this great political literature of historical significance.

Taipei, Taiwan
November 12, 1953

Chia-luen Lo.

# 英文三民主義節本序 羅家倫

　　剷除繼續到四千餘年的君主專制政體，他是世界上歷史最長久的一個，而建立中華民國，他更是遠東第一個民主共和國，這偉大工作的完成者就是　孫逸仙博士。他是一位偉大的革命領袖，但是他不祇是革命領袖；他是大思想家，是有遠大眼光和崇高理想的政治家。當他從事革命的初期，他早已認清社會民主和經濟民主是不可抵抗的力量，必須把他們合併到廣義的、民族革命的計劃裏面來。他更體會到，若是政治的權力，社會的公道，和經濟的平等三者不能得到妥善的配合，則任何國民革命運動的成就，都是白費氣力的，因為不如此首先就不能得到國家的安定和繁榮。因此他是中華民族第一領導者，能把三民主義、民主政治、和社會經濟的民主思想，融合為一整體，是為「三民主義」。這是他自己的政治和社會哲學的系統，也就是今天愛好自由的中國人所遵守的指導原則。

　　孫博士有希臘大哲蘇格拉底的習慣，隨時隨地發揮他思想的系統，而並無事前準備的講稿。他是一位動人的演說家，「信口拈來，都成妙諦」，有時更常用通俗的詞句，加以反復的說明，乃至夾入淺顯的故事，總期適合聽眾高低不同的知識水準，得到他所希望的心理反應。這本「三民主義」就是根據民國十三年他在廣東高等師範學校講演的記錄編印成書的。他原來計劃把其中每一主義，作六篇演講，但是講到最後將完的時候，因督師北伐，竟無暇將民生主義的最末兩講講完。最近我很高興的知道他的大弟子　蔣總統介石，添寫了講「育」和「樂」的兩篇，以完成這都偉大著作的未竟之功。

　　因為這部原書所根據是當時演講的記錄，所以原書的譯者畢範宇博士在他的譯序裏，說明他在翻譯時遇着了許多困難，如演講時「為引起聽衆注意而常加重複的解釋，和中國口話中常有在文法上鬆散的句法，以致原文的組織，不免過長。」現在這部畢譯的節本，乃是根據最近臺北中央文物供應社出版的中文節本，由曹文彥教授對照節錄而成的。節錄後文字頗覺緊湊，氣勢也較流暢，更容易引起他國讀者的興趣，而能增加他們對於中國革命原動力的了解。

　　自從　孫博士發表這本系統的演講到現在，中國國內的和國際間的政治、軍事同經濟的情形，都經過了重大的變化。有些適合那時期的情況和情緒的字句與章節，到現在自然仍保持着歷史上的價值。存着這種歷史的眼光，則讀者對於這部在歷史上有重要性的偉大政治文獻，便能得到更深層的了解，和更進一步的讚揚。

## DR. SUN YAT-SEN'S WILL

For forty years I have devoted myself to the cause of the people's revolution with but one end in view, the elevation of China to a position of freedom and equality among the nations. My experiences during these forty years have firmly convinced me that to attain this goal we must bring about a thorough awakening of our own people and ally ourselves in a common struggle with those peoples of the world who treat us on the basis of equality.

The work of the Revolution is not yet done. Let all our comrades follow my *Plans for National Reconstruction, Fundamentals of National Reconstruction, Three Principles of the People,* and the *Manifesto* issued by the First National Convention of our Party, and strive on earnestly for their consummation. Above all, our recent declarations in favor of the convocation of a National Convention and the abolition of unequal treaties should be carried into effect with the least possible delay. This is my heartfelt charge to you.

(Signed) SUN WEN
MARCH 11, 1925

*Written on February 20, 1925*

# 總 理 遺 囑

余致力國民革命，凡四十年，其目的在求中國之自由平等，積四十年之經驗，深知欲達到此目的，必須喚起民衆，及聯合世界上以平等待我之民族，共同奮鬥！

現在革命尚未成功，凡我同志，務須依照余所著建國方略，建國大綱，三民主義及第一次全國代表大會宣言，繼續努力，以求貫徹，最近主張開國民會議及廢除不平等條約，尤須於最短期間促其實現，是所至囑！

# TRANSLATOR'S PREFACE

This translation of "*San Min Chu I*"* is made from the tenth edition of the Chinese book issued by the Commercial Press in May, 1927. The text in recent editions is more accurate, as several typographical errors of earlier editions have been corrected.

The extemporaneous style of Dr. Sun's lectures, the constant repetition for sake of emphasis and the looseness of Chinese Pai-hua (spoken language) construction make the original quite a lengthy book. A complete translation will seem redundant to many Western readers; yet it has seemed wise, in view of the prominent and influential place which *The Three Principles of the People* holds in the Chinese Nationalist movement and because of the difficulty involved in making a fair selection of passages for an abridged edition, to translate the entire book. A full translation will also be of assistance, I hope, to some Westerners who are reading the book in Chinese and to Chinese students who are interested to know English equivalents for Dr. Sun's phrases and terms.

I have tried to make the translation faithful to the original and yet clear to the English reader. This is not an easy task, as many terms and expressions do not have exact English equivalents and a phrase is frequently used in different senses. *Mints'u* for example, is used by Dr.

* Literally, "Three-People-Principles." The last two syllables are pronounced like "joo-ee."

Sun in the sense of nation, nationality, or race, depending upon the context. *Ch'uan* sometimes means sovereignty, sometimes right, and at other times power or authority. Some terms have been transliterated as well as translated. Quotation marks usually mean that a Chinese idiom or proverb has been literally translated.

The generally accepted Romanization of familiar Chinese proper names has been followed; the Wade system has been used in the spelling of all other names. Geographical and historical references have been verified as far as possible.

Three features not in the original Chinese text have been added in the translation, for which the translator assumes full responsibility. The number of paragraphs has been increased. A few brief notes have been added to explain generally unfamiliar names and references. And in order to facilitate a rapid survey of the book and reference to various passages, a brief summary has been placed at the beginning of each chapter.*

Many friends have aided in the production of this translation. Mr. L. T. Chen has edited it and has written an introductory biographical sketch of Dr. Sun Yat-sen. Dr. Fong F. Sec has taken a deep interest in the work and has given many valuable suggestions. I am especially indebted to Mr. Ho Ping-song (何炳松), formerly professor of history at the Peking National University and now head of the Chinese Literature Department of the Commercial Press, for his thorough and painstaking revision of the translation. His cooperation has been invaluable. The proof pages have been read by Mrs. O. D. Rasmussen and

* In this abridged form of the book, the brief summary placed at the beginning of each chapter is left out.

by Miss Alice M. Roberts of the Commercial Press staff, by Rev. Frank R. Millican, who has made a careful study of the Chinese text, and by my Hangchow College colleague, Professor C. B. Day. My wife helped me in the preparation of the typewritten copy for the press.

This translation is issued under the auspices of the China Committee, Institute of Pacific Relations, as a volume of the "International Understanding Series," with the hope that it will promote a better understanding abroad of the great forces that are now driving China forward.

FRANK W. PRICE

*Shanghai, August, 1927.*

# 序

畢 範 宇

本書之迻譯，係以民國十六年五月商務印書館印行之三民主義（中文本）第十版為依據。該書係新近印行之版本，已將前幾版若干誤排之處，加以改正，故較為正確。

孫中山先生以卽席演說方式所為之演講，往往為加強語氣而反覆申述，且因白話語辭結構之疎鬆，遂使原本文字頗為冗長。若全部譯出，對於西方讀者，似嫌累贅，惟以三民主義對於中國國民黨革命運動影響之大與夫刪節本選擇之不易，遂譯全文，似不失為明智之舉。我希望全文譯本對於閱讀中文本之西方讀者有所幫助，而對於中國學生欲瞭解中山先生所用語辭之英文術語者，亦有所裨益也。

譯者曾盡力使譯文信達，而為西方讀者所瞭解。惟此事實非易易。蓋以若干中文語辭尚無確當之同義英文語辭，且同一名辭常被用於數種不同之義意上。舉例言之：「民族」一辭，必須視其文義而定其涵義，或作「民族」解，或作「國民」解，或作「種族」解。「權」之一辭，有時作「主權」解，有時作「權利」解，更有時作「權力」或「權威」等解。有些語辭遂用音譯直譯，而若干中國成語及格言則以直譯方法譯出，另加引號。

中國專有名詞（如人名地名等）為衆所習知者，採用通行之羅馬拼音，至其他專有名詞，則採用韋德制。有關史地之參考資料，則盡其可能，加以引證。

本書有三特點，而為原本所無者，譯者願負全責，卽一為譯文分段、分節，較原文為增多，一為罕見名詞及參考資料，附以簡注，一為使讀者易於速檢全書及查閱章節，於每篇之首，冠以提要。（編者註：此項篇首提要，經已刪去。）

　　本書之成，多承友人之賜助。陳立廷先生參與編輯，並爲本書撰孫中山先生傳略。鄺富灼博士對此事至感興趣，並提供許多寶貴建議，前國立北京大學史學敎授現任商務印書館中國文學部主任何炳松先生，曾予以縝密辛勤之校訂，此譯者所尤深感謝者。何氏之合作，實極可貴。校對工作，係由商務印書館 Mrs. O. D. Rasmussen, Miss Alice M. Roberts 及 Frank R. Millican 牧師及之江文理學院同事 C. B. Day 敎授等擔任。而 Frank R. Millican 牧師則於中文原本曾精爲核對。內子則協助打字，以備付印。

　　本書承太平洋關係學會中國分會之贊助，列爲國際知識叢書之一，期能增進國外人士對此復興中國之偉大力量，獲一更深之瞭解。（編者附註：此文原係畢範宇先生以英文寫出，茲經編者譯爲中文，特此註明）。

## AUTHOR'S PREFACE

After the three volumes of my *Plans for National Reconstruction—Psychological Reconstruction, Material Reconstruction, Social Reconstruction*—had been published,* I devoted myself to the writing of *Reconstruction of the State*, in order to complete the series. This book, which was larger than the former three volumes, included *The Principle of Nationalism, The Principle of Democracy, The Principle of Livelihood, The Quintuple-Power Constitution, Local Government, Central Government, Foreign Policy, National Defense*, altogether eight parts. Part One, *The Principle of Nationalism*, had already gone to press; the other two parts on democracy and livelihood were almost completed while the general line of thought and method of approach in the other parts had already been mapped out. I was waiting, for some spare time in which I might take up my pen and, without much further research, proceed with the writing. Just as I was contemplating the completion and publication of the book, Ch'en Ch'iungming unexpectedly revolted, on June 16, 1922, and turned his guns upon Kwan-yin Shan.** My notes and manuscripts which represented the mental labor of years and hundreds of foreign books which I had collected for reference were all destroyed by fire. It was a distressing loss.

It now happens that the Kuomintang is being re-

* In 1918.
** A hill in Canton near the headquarters of Dr. Sun.

xiv

organized and our comrades are beginning to engage in a
determined attack upon the minds of our people. They
are in great need of the profound truths of *San Min Chu I*
and the important ideas in the *The Quintuple-Power Constitution* as material for publicity. So I have been de-
livering one lecture a week. Mr. Hwang Ch'ang-ku is
making stenographic reports of the lectures and Mr. Tsou
Lu is revising them. The *Principle of Nationalism* series
has just been completed and is being published first in a
single volume as a gift to our comrades. In these lectures
I do not have the time necessary for careful preparation
nor the books necessary for reference. I can only mount
the platform and speak extemporaneously, and so am really
leaving out much that was in my former manuscripts.
Although I am making additions and corrections before
sending the book to the press, yet I realize that in clear
presentation of the theme in orderly arrangement of the
discussion and in the use of supporting facts, these lectures
are not at all comparable to the material which I had
formerly prepared. I hope that all our comrades will
take the book as a basis or as a stimulus, expand and correct
it, supply omissions, improve the arrangement and make
it a perfect text for publicity purposes. Then the benefits which it will bring to our people and to our state will
truly be immeasurable.

SUN WEN

*Canton, March 30, 1924.*

# 自　序

　　自建國方畧之心理建設、物質建設、社會建設三書出版之後，予乃從事於草作國家建設，以完成此帙。國家建設一書，較前三書爲獨大，內涵有民族主義、民權主義、民生主義、五權憲法、地方政府、中央政府、外交政策、國防計畫八冊。而民族主義一冊，已經脫稿，民權主義、民生主義二冊，亦草就大部，其他各冊於思想之綫索，研究之門徑，亦大畧規畫就緒，俟有餘暇，便可執筆直書，無待思索，方擬全書告竣，乃出而問世，不期十一年六月十六陳烱明叛變，砲擊觀音山，竟將數年心血所成之各種草稿，並備參考之西籍數百種，悉被燬去，殊可痛恨。

　　兹值國民黨改組，同志決心從事攻心之奮闘，亟需三民主義之奧義，五權憲法之要旨，爲宣傳之資。故於每星期演講一次。由黃昌穀君筆記之，由鄒魯君讀校之。今民族主義適已講完，特先印單行本，以饗同志。惟此次演講，旣無暇晷以預備，又無書籍爲參考，只於登壇之後，隨意發言，較之前稿，遺忘實多，雖於付梓之先，復加刪補，然於本題之精義，與敍論之條理，及印證之事實，都覺遠不如前。尙望同志讀者，本此基礎，觸類引伸，匡補闕遺，更正條理，使成爲一完善之書，以作宣傳之課本，則其造福於吾民族、吾國家，誠未可限量也。民國十三年三月三十日孫文序於廣州大本營。

## BIOGRAPHICAL SKETCH OF

## DR. SUN YAT-SEN

Dr. Sun Yat-sen, founder of the Chinese Republic and leader of the Revolution, was born of peasant parentage on November 12, 1866, in a little village near Hsiangshan, a small city in the province of Kwangtung. Here he spent an uneventful childhood attending the village school with the children of the neighborhood. At thirteen years of age he made a trip to Honolulu, where he remained for five years and completed his high school course. There he breathed the spirit of liberty and absorbed freely the influences of American life. When he returned, therefore, to Hongkong and entered Queen's College, he was already dissatisfied with the political life of his own beloved country. Graduating at the age of twenty, he undertook to prepare himself for the medical profession and completed his training in the Hongkong Medical College in the year 1892.

His professional practice, however, was short-lived, for he gave it up to respond to a higher call following China's defeat in the Sino-Japanese War (1894-1895). This was by no means a new enthusiasm but rather a forward step in the career which he had chosen early in his college days. Every day he spent in Hongkong under British rule and every defeat China suffered at the hands of other countries added vigor to his conviction that the

government of his own country was rotten to the core.
Nothing short of a revolution would provide the remedy.
He had dedicated himself to this cause, and among his
fellow students he had found a few with whom he could
share his deepest aspirations. The task of building up a
free and enlightened China became his sole purpose in
life.

From the very beginning the undertaking was fraught
with dangers. After a hasty attempt at revolt that failed,
he embarked in 1895 on his life of exile. Pursued by personal danger he went first to Japan, then to America, and
was finally kidnapped on the streets of London and carried
off to the Chinese legation, where he was kept hidden for
twelve days. Thanks to the loyalty and ingenuity of his
friend Dr. James Cantlie he escaped, and the scheme to
smuggle him back to China for execution came to naught.
He proceeded to Europe and spent the next few years
studying the social and political institutions in the countries
he visited. During this time he formulated his *Three
Principles of the People* and spread his gospel of revolution among his compatriots wherever he went.

After the Boxer trouble in 1900, the cause of the Revolution gained in momentum. The overthrow of the
Manchu regime had become a definite program and large
numbers of Chinese men and women in all parts of the
world joined in the crusade. A conference was held in
Tokyo in 1905, at which two important resolutions were
passed: (1) that the Revolutionists be united under the
name of the Tung Meng Hui, and (2) that the reigning
dynasty be deposed and China transformed into a republic.
The membership of the conference included representatives from all the provinces of China and numerous persons

from the ranks of Chinese merchants in other lands. The former engaged themselves in an active campaign of secret propaganda in the homeland and the latter opened their purses in unstinted support of these efforts. But for the generous giving of these patriotic businessmen abroad it is improbable that the Revolution could have materialized.

The culmination of these efforts came in the autumn of 1911, when the battle cry was sounded in Wuchang. This capital of Hupeh quickly fell to the Revolutionists. Although the outbreak was precipitated by mistake before the plans were completed, the response in other parts of the country was so widespread that the Revolution was a *fait accompli* in less than one hundred days! The effete Manchu government was overthrown, and Dr. Sun's dream of years had become a reality. His undaunted spirit had won the day and his weary body had earned a momentary rest. He was called upon, however, to become the first president of the new Republic, and hopes ran high that a rejuvenated China would turn a new page in history.

But the events of 1911 proved to be only the beginning of a long process. Broadly speaking, two schools of thinking came to dominate the minds of young China, the one led by Yuan Shih-kai and the other by Sun Yat-sen. The former believed in military force, the latter pinned his hope on the awakening of the masses of the people. In order that he might better accomplish his purpose, Dr. Sun yielded the presidency to Yuan after he had held it for only three months. He chose to devote himself to the task of educating the people to an understanding of the fundamentals of democracy and of uplifting their economic standards. The Tung Meng Hui was reorganized as a political party with a broader program under the name

Kuomintang, and a nation-wide plan of railroad building
was undertaken as the first step towards the industrializa-
tion of the country. But the personal ambition of Yuan
Shih-kai interfered. Instead of giving himself unselfishly
to the political reconstruction of the country, he saw in the
situation an opportunity for self-aggrandizement. He dis-
regarded Parliament and set out to make himself emperor.
Dr. Sun realized too late that his confidence had been mis-
placed and that the Revolution had been smothered by
treason.

This fatal mistake delayed the Revolution until the
autumn of 1926, when Chiang Kai-shek finally stepped into the shoes of his deceased leader and led the Nationalist
forces on their victorious march from Canton toward the
north. Yuan meanwhile had left a legacy of militaristic
oppression under which China continues to groan.

But it would be a mistake to think that these sixteen
years following the initial success of the Revolution were
wasted. Dr. Sun's untiring efforts guided the people of
China into a constantly growing patriotism and national
consciousness. He attracted to his side many leaders and
numberless patriots eager to undertake the task of carrying
on the Revolution to a finish. The more he met with
reverses the stronger became his hold on his followers.
Several times he set up a separate government in Canton
and as often his plans were frustrated, until finally in 1923
a stable regime was established and a demonstration of
efficient and effective government was made. During this
period he reorganized the Kuomintang for the third time
and made clear the practice of party government. He
elaborated his political philosophy of the Three Principles
in a series of popular lectures, and sounded the clarion call

with respect to the unequal treaties. These achievements constitute the basic ideals and policies of the Revolutionary movement. The Three Principles inspired the people with a political ideal, and the denunciation of the unequal treaties released a latent force in the hearts of the people nurtured by the inarticulate desires of many years. Dr. Sun Yat-sen was a diligent student, a farsighted statesman, an indefatigable worker, an irrepressible optimist and, above all, he was China's beloved leader, clear of vision and steadfast in purpose. He not only blazed the trail in the reconstruction of new China, but he also laid down the highways leading towards the successful consummation of his ideals in the future. Out of his years of trial and travail he discovered for coming generations a sure way for the recovery of national freedom.

On March 12, 1925, when the unification of China was apparently within reach, he died in Peking. For a short while rumors were rife reporting the disintegration of the party which he had founded and had taken pains to build up. But the fact was quickly revealed that the party was stronger than ever after his death. His indestructible spirit gripped the lives of his followers even more powerfully than before. It is sometimes even suggested that his death has actually served to accelerate the progress of the Revolution.

But in the thinking of Dr. Sun the Revolution is a continuous process. This " period of military achievement " represents only its beginning and is of less importance than the " period of training " which is to follow. Only when the training process is completed can the Revolution bring the country to the full enjoyment of democracy. In his own words uttered on his deathbed, " The Revolution is not yet completed. All my comrades must strive on."

Dr. Sun died a comparatively poor man, leaving behind no property except a house which his adherents overseas had bought for him over ten years ago, and a library said to be one of the best on social and political sciences in existence. For forty years he toiled " in order to achieve freedom and equality from China." He is the father of new China, taking his place among the foremost leaders in history.

L. T. CHEN

*Shanghai, 1927.*

# 孫中山先生傳略　　陳立廷

中華民國創造者，革命領袖　孫中山先生於民國紀元前四十六年（清同治五年西元一八六六年）十一月十二日誕生於廣東省香山縣（即今之中山縣）翠亨村農家。幼年與隣童入村塾讀書，年十三赴檀香山旅居五年，完成其中學學程。並在該地吸取自由之精神，大受美國生活之影響。自檀島囘里後，即入香港皇仁書院肄業。對當時政治已不滿意。年二十畢業於皇仁書院。嗣決投身習醫，於民國前二十年（西元一八九二年）完成其學業於香港西醫書院。

先生執醫業爲時甚暫，蓋以甲午之役（西元一八九四至一八九五年）中國爲日本所敗，　先生遂棄醫業而從事革命工作。此非由於當時一時熱忱所激動，蓋其於求學時即矢志從事於革命，此不過其事業之初步耳。時　先生在英人統治下之香港，每值清廷受挫於列强，益感滿清政府之腐敗，含革命外無他策。　先生乃委身於革命並從其同學中，覓得志同道合者數人。其畢業生唯一志願在求建立一自由開明之中國。

當革命事業開始之際，險象環生，民國前十七年（清光緒二十一年，西元一八九五年）倉卒舉義於廣州，以事機洩露，遂告失敗，　先生乃渡海出走，先赴日本，繼往美洲，復至英國，終在倫敦街上被誘禁於中國公使館，經十二日之久，幸經英人康德黎博士竭智盡力爲之營救，始得脫險，清廷密謀運送　先生囘國治罪之惡計，卒未得酬。此後數年　先生漫游歐陸，考察各國社會政治設施，在此期間揭櫫其三民主義之學說，履及之處，並將其革命主義傳播於各地之僑胞。

民國前十二年（光緒二十六年，西元一九〇〇年），經義和團擾亂後，革命之進行，逐漸加速。推翻滿清統治，成爲明確之計劃，海內外仁人志士，無分男女，聞風興起，紛紛踴躍參加革命行列。民國前七年（光緒三十一年，西元一九○五年）在日本東京舉行集會，獲致二項重要決議：一爲併合各革命團體於同盟會，一爲推翻滿清締造共和。當時與會同志，包括各省代表及國外各地有財力人士，前者在國內從事於積極之秘密宣傳運動，後者則踴躍捐款支助革命。若非海外愛國僑商，慷慨解囊，革命偉業，恐無實現之可能。

革命行動至 民國前一年秋間（辛亥，宣統三年，西元一九一一年）已臻頂點。武昌義旗一舉，不旋踵間，此湖北省會即爲革命軍所佔領。雖然武昌發難事起非常，但全國各省，聞風響應，不及百日，而革命告成。清祚旣屋， 先生若干年來夢寐以求者乃得實現。 先生之大無畏精神贏得勝利，而疲憊之身遂獲片刻之休憩。次年 先生被推選爲中華民國第一任大總統。行見新生之中國，將展開歷史之新頁，寄予無限之希望焉。

惟辛亥之役僅爲艱巨革命事業之開端。概言之，當時有兩派思想存在於少年中國之心中，一爲袁世凱所領導之思想，一爲 中山先生所領導之思想，前者迷信武力，後者希望喚醒民衆。 先生爲欲完成其志願，就任未及三月，即讓位於袁。乃周遊各省，宣傳主義，敎育民衆使了解民主政治之本質，並謀國民經濟水準之提高。嗣改組同盟會，爲具有宏大政綱之政黨，定名國民黨，並着手計劃全國鐵路建設，以爲促進全國實業化之初步。但袁世凱爲野心所迷，不圖國家政治之建設，而妄欲乘機坐大，視國會若無睹，並着手自建朝廷，竊據九五。迨 中山先生洞悉所託非人，惜爲時已晚而革命幾被叛逆所斲喪矣。

由於袁世凱叛國，遂使革命之完成，爲之遲滯甚久，彼所遺留軍閥專制之餘毒，迫使中國遭受頻年戰亂之痛苦。直至民國十五年秋，蔣公中正，秉 中山先生之遺志，率師北伐，由穗而上，底定南北。

自革命初步成功以還，十六年之時間，並未虛擲。 中山先生不斷之努力，領導國民，激發其日益增長之愛國良知，與民族意識。不少社會首領與無數愛國志士受其感召，皆集於 先生之左右，熱望繼續革命巨業，使其底於完成。遭遇愈逆而團結愈堅。數度在穗組織政府，其計劃亦數度受挫。最後至民國十二年穩固之政權遂告建立，强有力之政府，因以實現。在此一時期內， 先生改組國民黨。建立政黨政治並精心詳述其三民主義之政治哲學，舉行有系統之演講，並大聲疾呼取銷不平等條約。上述各項成就皆構成革命運動之基本理想與政策。三民主義以一種政治理想感召國人，廢除不平等條約之主張，則使若干年來蘊藏國人內心之潛在力量，得以激發無遺。 中山先生為一嗜學不厭之學者，目光遠大之政治家，不厭不倦之實行家，不屈不撓之樂觀者，尤要者，為全國愛戴之領袖，觀察確實而意志堅定。先生不僅畢生盡瘁革命重建新中國，亦且為他日達到其成功之理想，闢就康莊大道，集多年之艱苦辛勤，為下一代恢復民族自由，發現一正確之途徑。

民國十四年三月十二日，當全國將趨統一之際， 先生逝世於北平，當時曾謠傳 先生辛勞手創之政黨行將趨於分裂，惟事實旋即證其非是。而自 先生逝世後，黨更趨堅強。 先生永不泯滅之精神，感召同志精誠團結，反較生前更甚。或竟謂 中山先生逝世後，革命之進行益形加速云。

依 先生之意見，革命實為一連續程序。「軍政時期」僅為革命程序之開始，而繼之以更為重要之「訓政時期」，訓政結束之後，革命方能登國民於民主政治袵席之上。 先生臨終時謂「革命尚未成功，同志仍須努力。」

中山先生平生無積蓄，遺產僅住宅一所，圖書館一處而已。其住宅係十餘年前海外同志集資購贈者，而圖書館則為當時收藏社會科學政治科學書籍最豐富者之一。 中山先生四十年之辛勤勞瘁，其目的在求中國之自由平等。國人尊 中山先生為新中國之國父。歷史上偉大袖領中 先生實占有崇高之地位。（編者附註：此文譯自陳立廷先生於民國十六年寫成之英文原著。）

# CONTENTS
## 目　　錄

# THE PRINCIPLE OF DEMOCRACY

# 民 權 主 義

## LECTURE ONE*

WHAT is the People's Sovereignty? In order to define this term we must first understand what a "people" is. Any unified and organized body of men is called a "people." What is "sovereignty"? It is power and authority extended to the area of the state. The states with the greatest power to-day are called in Chinese the "strong states," in foreign languages the "powers." Mechanical force is spoken of in Chinese as "horse strength," in other languages as "horse power." Thus strength and power are used interchangeably. The power to execute orders and to regulate public conduct is called "sovereignty," and when "people" and "sovereignty" are linked together, we have the political power of the people. To understand "political power" we must know what government is. Many people

* Delivered on March 9, 1924.

## 第 一 講

民國十三年三月九日講

甚麼叫做民權主義呢？現在要把民權來定一個解釋。便先要知道甚麼是民。大凡有團體有組織的衆人就叫做民。甚麼是權呢？權就是力量，就是威勢，那些力量大到同國家一樣，就叫做權。力量最大的那些國家，中國話說列強，外國話便說列權。又機器的力量，中國話說是馬力，外國話說是馬權，所以權和力實在是相同。有行使命令的力量，有制服羣倫的力量，就叫做權。把民同權合攏起來說，民權就是人民的政治力量。甚麼是叫做政治的力量呢？我們要明白這個道理，便先要明白甚麼是政治，許多人以爲政治是

1

think that government is a very abstruse and difficult subject which ordinary persons cannot comprehend. Chinese military men are always saying, "We are soldiers and know nothing about politics." The reason why they are ignorant is that they consider government to be a deep and abstruse study. They do not know that it is a very clear and comprehensible thing. If military men say that they will not interfere with government, we can let them by; but if they say that they cannot understand government, they are foolish. Since the soldier is the driving force behind the government, he should certainly understand what government is. Briefly, government is a thing of the people and by the people; it is control of the affairs of all the people. The power of control is political sovereignty, and where the people control the government we speak of the "people's sovereignty."

Now that we understand what the "people's sovereignty" is, we must study its functions. As we view life about us or study into the distant past, we see that human power has been employed, to put it simply, in maintaining the existence of the human race. In order to exist, mankind must have protection and sustenance and it is daily engaged in meeting these two

很奧妙艱深的東西,是通常人不容易明白的。所以中國的軍人常常說,我們是軍人,不懂得政治。爲甚麼不懂得政治呢?就是因爲他們把政治看作是很奧妙很艱深的,殊不知道政治是很淺白很明瞭的,如果軍人說不干涉政治,還可以講得通,但是說不懂得政治,便講不通了,因爲政治的原動力便在軍人,所以軍人當然要懂得政治,要明白甚麼是政治。政治兩字的意思,淺而言之,政就是衆人的事,治就是管理,管理衆人的事便是政治。有管理衆人之事的力量,便是政權。今以人民管理政事,便叫做民權。

現在民權的定義,旣然是明白了,便要研究民權是甚麼作用的。環觀近世,追溯往古,權的作用,簡單的說,就是要來維持人類的生存。人類要能夠生存,就須有兩件最大的事:第一件是保,第二件是養。保和養兩件大事,是人類天天要做的。保

2

great needs. Protection means self-defense: whether it is an individual or a group or a state, the power of self-defense is necessary to existence. Sustenance means seeking food. Self-defense and food-seeking are, then, the two chief means by which mankind maintains its existence. But while man is maintaining his existence, other animals are also trying to maintain theirs; while man is defending himself, other animals are also defending themselves; while man seeks food, other animals are also seeking food; and so the protection and the sustenance of man comes into conflict with the protection and the sustenance of other animals, and struggle ensues. To keep alive in the midst of struggle man must fight, and so mankind has not ceased to fight since the beginning of human life. Thus the human race has used its strength in combat, and since its birth upon the planet until now has lived in the thick of strife.

While the germs of democracy were found in Greece and Rome two thousand years ago, yet only within the last one hundred fifty years has democracy become firmly rooted in the world. The preceding age was one of autocracy and the age before that one of theocracy. Before theocracy came the wilderness age when men fought with

就是自衛,無論是個人或團體或國家,要有自衛的能力,才能夠生存。養就是覓食。這自衛和覓食,便是人類維持生存的兩件大事。但是人類要維持生存,他項動物也要維持生存,人類要自衛,他項動物,也要自衛,人類要覓食,他項動物也要覓食,所以人類的保養和動物的保養衝突,便發生競爭。人類要在競爭中求生存,便要奮鬪,所以奮鬪這一件事,是自有人類以來天天不息的。由此便知權是人類用來奮鬪的,人類由初生以至於現在,天天都是在奮鬪之中。

民權之萌芽,雖在二千年前之希臘羅馬時代,但是確立不搖,只有一百五十年,前此仍是君權時代。君權之前便是神權時代,而神權之前,便是洪荒時代。在那個時候,人類要圖

3

beasts. Man sought to live and the animal sought to live. Man had two ways of preserving his existence —through seeking food and through self-defense. In very ancient times men ate beasts and beasts also ate men; there was a constant struggle between them. The land was covered with venomous snakes and wild animals; man was beset by dangers and so had to fight for his very life. The warfare of that day was the irregular conflict between man and beast; there was no banding into groups, it was "each fighting for himself."

In the primitive struggle between man and wild beasts, man used only his individual physical strength or sometimes the species would fight together; if, for instance, in one place a few score men were battling with a few score beasts, and in another place, another group of men were doing the same thing, the men of both places might perceive their own kinship to each other and their difference from the animals, unite as fellow creatures, and fight together against the other species. Certainly man would not join with another species to fight and devour man and injure his own kind. Such a banding together of the species and unwitting alliance against reptiles and beasts was a natural, not an artificial thing; when the reptiles

生存，獸類也要圖生存。人類保全生存的方法，一方面是覓食，一方面是自衛。在太古時代，人食獸，獸亦食人，彼此相競爭，遍地都是毒蛇猛獸，人類的四周都是禍害，所以人類要圖生存，便要去奮鬥。但是那時的奮鬥，總是人獸到處混亂的奮鬥，不能結合得大團體，所謂各自為戰。

古時人同獸鬥，只有用個人的體力，在那個時候，只有同類相助。比方在這個地方有幾十個人同幾十個猛獸奮鬥，在別的地方也有幾十個人同幾十個猛獸奮鬥，這兩個地方的人類，見得彼此都是同類的，和猛獸是不同的，於是同類的互相集合起來，和不同類的去奮鬥，決沒有和不同類的動物集合，共同來食人的，來殘害同類的。當時同類的集合，不約而同去打那些毒蛇猛獸，那種集合是天然的，不是人為的，把毒蛇猛獸打完了，各人還是散去。因

or beasts were destroyed the men scattered. At that time there was no such thing as popular sovereignty; man, in fighting the animals, used simply his own physical prowess and not any kind of authority. It was an age of brute force.

Later, when man had about extermniated the venomous reptiles and savage beasts, when his environment was somewhat improved, and his dwelling place was better suited to his type of existence, then groups of people began to live in one place and to domesticate the tamer animals. This was the beginning of the pastoral age and also of civilization. A great change now took place in man's living conditions: warfare with animals was about at an end, civilization was growing up, what we call the ancient period of human history had arrived. Man began to direct his warfare against the forces of Nature. Briefly, in the first stage man warred with beasts and employed his own brute force or the united strength of many to kill them off; in the second stage man warred with Nature. In the first stage, because man did not know when an animal would attack him, he was not sure whether he could live from one moment to another; he had

為當時民權沒有發生，人類去打那些毒蛇猛獸，各人都是各用氣力，不是用權力，所以在那個時代，人同獸爭，是用氣力的時代。

後來毒蛇猛獸差不多都被人殺完了，人類所處的環境較好，所住的地方極適於人類的生存，人羣就住在一處，把馴伏的禽獸養起來，供人類的使用，故人類把毒蛇猛獸殺完了之後，便成畜牧時代，也就是人類文化初生的時代。到了那個時代，人類生活的情形，便發生一個大變動。所以人同獸鬥終止，便是文化初生，這個時代可以叫做太古時代。到了那個時代，人又同甚麼東西去奮鬥呢？是同天然物力去奮鬥。簡而言之，世界進化，當第一個時期，是人同獸爭，所用的是氣力，大家同心協力，殺完毒蛇猛獸。第二個時期，是人同天爭。在人同獸爭的時代，因為不知道何時有毒蛇猛獸來犯，所以人類時時刻刻不知生死，所有的自衛力只有雙手雙足。不

only his two hands and two feet for self-defense, but he was wiser than the beasts and learned to use sticks and stones for weapons, so finally he won a complete victory over his wild enemies. Only then could man plan ahead for a day; while he was battling with the beasts his life was not secure for a moment.

When wild beasts no longer threatened, the human race began to multiply and the most favorable spots on the earth began to fill up with people. What were the favorable spots?—Places sheltered from wind and rain or regions which storms did not touch.

After driving out the poisonous reptiles and savage beasts they were faced with natural disasters of storm and flood. Naturally they would try to avert these disasters and to struggle against Nature. In the age of warfare with the beasts man could use his own physical strength to fight, but mere fighting was of no value in the day of struggle against Nature. Mankind then suffered many hardships until some wise men came forth with schemes for the welfare of the people. Thus the Great Yu* reduced the waters to order and averted the calamity of flood for

* The first emperor of the Hsia.

6

過在那個時候，人要比獸聰明些，所以同獸奮鬥，不是專用雙手雙足，還曉得用木棍和石頭。故最後的結果，人類戰勝，把獸類殺滅淨盡，人類的生命，才可以一天一天的計算。在人同獸鬥的時期，人類的安全，幾幾乎一時一刻都不能保。

到了沒有獸類的禍害，人類才逐漸蕃盛，好地方都被人住滿了，當那個時代，甚麼是叫做好地方呢？可以避風雨的地方，便叫做好地方，就是風雨所不到的地方。

在這個地方，驅完毒蛇猛獸之後，便有天災，便要受風雨的禍患。遇到天災，人類要免去那種災害，便要與天爭。說到人同獸爭的時代，人類還可用氣力去打，到了同天爭的時代，專講打是不可能的，故當時人類感覺非常的困難。後來便有聰明的人出來，替人民謀幸福，像大禹治水，替人民除去水患。有巢氏敎民在樹上做居室，替人民謀避風雨的災害。

the people, and Yu Ch'ao Shih (the Nest Builder)* taught the people how to build houses in trees and avert the disasters from wind and storm.

From this time on civilization slowly progressed, the people began to unite, and, as land was plentiful and the inhabitants were few, food was very easy to procure. The only problems were the catastrophes of Nature which could not be fought, as the wild beasts were, with bodily strength, and so there arose the idea of divine power. Men of deep wisdom began to advocate the doctrine of gods and divine teachings, and introduced prayers as a means of warding off evil and obtaining blessings. There was no way of telling at the time whether their praying was effective or not; however, since they were struggling against Heaven they had no other plan, when in extremity, but to appeal for the power of the gods. A man of profound insight would be chosen as leader, like the chiefs of savage tribes in Africa today, whose special duty it was to offer prayers. In the same way Mongolians and Tibetans now make a "Living Buddha" their ruler and are under a religious government. So the ancients used to say that the two great functions of the state

* Legendary ruler of ancient Chinese history.

自此以後，文化便逐漸發達，人民也逐漸團結起來。又因為當時地廣人稀，覓食很容易，他們單獨的問題，只有天災，所以要和天爭。但是和天爭不比是和獸爭，可以用氣力的，於是發生神權。極聰明的人，便提倡神道設教，用祈禱的方法去避禍求福。他們所做祈禱的工夫，在當時是或有效或無效，是不可知。但是既同天爭，無法之中，是不得不用神權，擁戴一個很聰明的人做首領，好比現在非洲野蠻的酋長，他的任務，便專是祈禱，又像中國的蒙古西藏，都奉活佛做皇帝，都是以神為治，所以古人說：「國之大事，在祀與戎」。說國家的大事，第一是祈禱，第二是打仗。

were worship and war, praying and fighting.

Thus after the age of warfare with wild animals came the struggles with Nature and out of these struggles was born theocracy. The next step in history was autocracy, when mighty warriors and political leaders wrested the power away from the religious rulers or put themselves at the head of the churches and appointed themselves kings. A period of struggle between man and man thus evolved. When struggles between man and man began to take the place of struggles with Nature, people realized that simple dependence upon the power of religious faith could neither protect society nor aid in warfare and that an enlightened government and strong military power were necessary in order to compete with other peoples. Men have fought against men since the beginning of recorded history. At first they employed both the power of religion and the power of autocracy in their struggles; later, as theocracy weakened and, after the dissolution of the Roman Empire, gradually decayed, autocracy became stronger until, in the reign of Louis XIV of France, it reached the peak of its power. Louis XIV said that there was no difference between the king and the state—"I

由此可見人同獸爭以後，便有天災，要和天爭，便發生神權。由有歷史到現在，經過神權之後，便發生君權。有力的武人和大政治家把教皇的權力奪了，或者自立為教主，或者自稱為皇帝。於是由人同天爭的時代，變成人同人爭。到了人同人相爭，便覺得單靠宗教的信仰力，不能維持人類社會，不能夠和人競爭，必要政治修明，武力强盛，才可以和別人競爭，世界自有歷史以來，都是人同人爭。從前人同人爭，一半是用神權，一半是用君權。後來神權漸少，羅馬分裂之後，神權漸衰，君權漸盛，到了法王路易十四，便為極盛的時代。他說：「皇帝和國家沒有分別，我是皇帝，所以我就是國家」。把國家的甚麼權都拿到自己手裏，專制到極點，好比中國秦始皇一樣。君主專制一天利害一天，弄到人民不能忍受。到了這個時代，科學也一天發達一天，人類的聰明

am the king, therefore I am the state." He took every power of the state into his own hands and exercised despotism to its limits, just as did Ch'in Shih Hwang* of China. The absolute monarchy became more terrible every day until the people could bear it no longer. About this time science was beginning to make steady progress and the general intelligence of mankind was steadily rising. As a result, a new consciousness was born. The people saw that autocracy was something that only grasped for power, made private property of the state and of the people, contributed to the gratification of one individual and did not care about the sufferings of the many; as it became unbearable they realized with increasing clearness that, since the system was iniquitous, they should resist it, and that resistance meant revolution. So, during the last hundred years, the tides of revolutionary thought have run high and have given rise to democratic revolutions, struggles between people and kings.

This division into periods will help us in studying the origins of democracy. Summing up: the first period was one of struggle between man and beast in which man employed physical strength rather than

---

* Despot who united China and founded the Ch'in dynasty (246-207 B.C.)

也一天進步一天，於是生出了一種大覺悟，知道君主總攬大權，把國家和人民做他一個人的私產，供他一個人的快樂，人民受苦他總不理會，人民到不能忍受的時候，便一天覺悟一天，知道君主專制是無道，人民應該要反抗，反抗就是革命，所以百餘年來，革命的思潮便非常發達，便發生民權的革命。民權革命，是誰同誰爭呢？就是人民同皇帝相爭。

所以推求民權的來源，我們可以用時代來分析。再概括的說一說：第一個時期，是人同獸爭，不是用權，是用氣力。第二個時期，是

9

any kind of power; in the second period man fought with Nature and called divine powers to his aid; in the third period, men came into conflict with men, states with states, races with races, and autocratic power was the chief weapon. We are now in the fourth period, of war within states, when the people are battling against their monarchs and kings. The issue now is between good and evil, between right and might, and as the power of the people is steadily increasing we may call this the age of the people's sovereignty—the age of democracy. This is a very new age. We have only recently entered upon it and overthrown the autocracy of the old age.

Is the change a good thing or not? When the masses were unenlightened and depended upon sacred kings and virtuous sages to lead them, autocracy was of considerable value. Before autocracies arose, holy men founded religion upon the way of the gods in order to conserve social values; at that time theocracy rendered a large service. But now autocracy and theocracy are things of the past and we have come to the age of democracy, the age of the people's power. Is there any just reason why we should oppose autocracy and insist upon democracy? Yes, because with the rapid

人同天爭，是用神權。第三個時期，是人同人爭，國同國爭，這個民族同那個民族爭，是用君權。到了現在的第四個時期，國內相爭，人民同君主相爭。在這個時代之中，可以說是善人同惡人爭，公理同強權爭。到這個時代，民權漸漸發達，所以叫做民權時代，這個時代是很新的。我們到了這個很新的時代，推倒舊時代的君權。

這究竟是好不好呢？從前人類的智識未開，賴有聖君賢相去引導，在那個時候，君權是很有用的。君權沒有發生以前，聖人以神道設教，去維持社會，在那個時候，神權也是很有用的。現在神權君權都是過去的陳跡，到了民權時代。就道理上講起來，究竟為甚麼反對君權，一定要用民權呢？因為近來文明很進步，人類的智識很發達，發生了大覺悟。好比我們在做小孩子的時候，便

advance of civilization people are growing in intelligence and developing a new consciousness of self, just as we, who as children wanted our parents to support us, cannot depend upon them further but must be independent when we grow up to manhood and seek our own living.

From two hundred thousand years up to ten or more thousand years ago, mankind lived under theocracy, and theocracy was well suited to the needs of the age. The situation in Europe was a similar one a thousand or more years ago. Chinese culture flowered earlier than European culture, so we have had more autocracy than theocracy; the age of autocracy began long ago in China. But the word democracy—popular sovereignty—has only lately been introduced into China. All of you who have come here today to support my revolution are naturally believers in democracy.

Which, autocracy or democracy, is really better suited to modern China? If we base our judgment upon the intelligence and the ability of the Chinese people, we come to the conclusion that the sovereignty of the people would be far more suitable for us. Confucius and Mencius two thousand years ago spoke for people's rights. Confucius said, "When the Great

要父母提攜，但是到了成人謀生的時候，便不能依靠父母，必要自己去獨立。

從二十萬年到萬幾千年以前，是用神權。神權很適宜於那個時代的潮流。歐洲幾千百年前也是這樣。中國文化發達的時期，早過歐洲，君權多過神權，所以中國老早便是君權時代。民權這個名詞，是近代傳進來的，大家今天來贊成我的革命，當然是主張民權的。

君權和民權，究竟是那一種適宜於現在的中國呢？根據中國人的聰明才智來講，如果應用民權，比較上還是適宜得多，所以兩千多年前的孔子、孟子，便主張民權。孔子說：「大道之行也，天下為公」。便是主張民權的大同世界。又「言必稱堯舜

Doctrine prevails, all under heaven will work for the common good."* He was pleading for a free and fraternal world in which the people would rule. He was constantly referring to Yao and Shun** simply because they did not try to monopolize the empire. Although their government was autocratic in name, yet in reality they gave the people power and so were highly reverenced by Confucius. Mencius said, "Most precious are the people; next come the land and grain; and last, the princes." Again: "Heaven sees as the people see, Heaven hears as the people hear," and "I have heard of the punishment of the tyrant Chou*** but never of the assassination of a sovereign." He, in his age, already saw that kings were not absolutely necessary and would not last forever, so he called those who brought happiness to the people holy monarchs, but those who were cruel and unprincipled he called individualists whom all should oppose. Thus China more than two millenniums ago had already considered the idea of democracy, but at that time she could not put it into operation. Democracy was then what foreigners call a

」。就是因為堯舜不是家天下。堯舜的政治，名義上雖然是用君權，實際上是行民權，所以孔子總是宗仰他們。孟子說「民為貴，社稷次之，君為輕」。又說：「天視自我民視，天聽自我民聽」。又說：「聞誅一夫紂矣，未聞弒君也」。他在那個時代，已經知道君主不必一定是要的，已經知道君主一定是不能長久的，所以便判定那些為民造福的就稱為「聖君」，那些暴虐無道的就稱為「獨夫」大家應該去反抗他。由此可見中國人對於民權的見解，二千多年以前，已經早想到了。不過那個時候，還以為不能做到，好像外國人說烏托邦，是理想上的事，不是即時可以做得到的。

* 天下為公  t'ien hsia wei kung.
** Legendary rulers of ancient Chinese history before Great Yu.
*** Last ruler of the Shang or Yin dynasty which fell 1121 B.C. A cruel tyrant condemned by all Chinese historians.

Utopia, an ideal which could not be immediately realized.

Now that Europe and America have founded republics and have applied democracy for one hundred fifty years, we whose ancients dreamed of these things should certainly follow the tide of world events and make use of the people's power if we expect our state to rule long and peacefully and our people to enjoy happiness. But the rise of democracy is comparatively recent and many states in the world are still autocratic; those which have tried democracy have experienced many disappoinments and failures. While democracy was discoursed upon in China two thousand years ago, it has become an accomplished fact for only one hundred fifty years in the West. Now it is suddenly spreading over the whole world on the wings of the wind.

The first instance of actual democracy in modern times was in England. A revolution of the people took place about the time of the close of the Ming dynasty and the beginning of the Manchu dynasty in China, under a leader named Cromwell, which resulted in the execution of King Charles I. This deed sent a thrill of horror through the people of Europe and America, who had never heard of the like in

現在歐美既是成立了民國，實現民權，有了一百五十年，中國古人也有這種思想，所以我們要希望國家長治久安，人民安樂，順乎世界的潮流，非用民權不可。但是民權發生，至今還不甚久，世界許多國家，還有用君權的。各國實行民權，也遭過了許多挫折，許多失敗的。民權言論的發生，在中國有了兩千多年，在歐美恢復民權，不過一百五十年，現在風行一時。

近代事實上的民權，頭一次發生是在英國，英國在那個時候發生民權革命，正當中國的明末清初。當時革命黨的首領，叫做格林威爾，把英國皇帝查理士第一殺了。此事發生以後，便驚動歐美一般人，以為這是自有歷史以來所沒有的，應該當作謀反叛逆看待。暗中弑君

the world before and who thought that those responsible should be treated as traitors and rebels. The secret assassination of princes was common in every country, but Cromwell's execution of Charles I was not done in secret; the king was given a public trial and openly proclaimed guilty of disloyalty to the state and to the people, and so deserving of death. Europe thought that the English people would defend the rights of the people, and give a great impetus to democracy, but, to the surprise of all, the English preferred autocracy to democracy; although Charles I was dead, they continued to long for a king. Within less than ten years the restoration of the monarchy had taken place and Charles II was welcomed back as king. This happened just at the time when the Manchus were entering the Great Wall, before the downfall of the Ming dynasty* not much further back than two hundred or more years. Something over two centuries ago, England had this one period of democratic government, but it soon collapsed and autocracy again held sway.

A hundred years later the American Revolution took place when the colonies broke away from England and declared independence, forming the federal government of the

* 1403-1644 A.D.

，各國是常有的，但是格林威爾殺查理士第一，不是暗殺，是把他拿到法庭公開裁判，宣佈他不忠於國家和人民的罪狀，所以便把他殺了。當時歐美以爲英國人民應該贊成民權，從此民權便可以發達。誰知英國人民還是歡迎君權，不歡迎民權，查理士第一雖然是死了，人民還是思慕君主。不到十年，英國便發生復辟，把查理士第二迎囘去做皇帝。那個時候，剛是滿清入關，明朝還沒有亡，距今不過兩百多年。所以兩百多年以前，英國發生過一次民權政治，不久便歸消滅，君權還是極盛。

一百年之後，便有美國的革命，脫離英國獨立，成立美國聯邦政府，到現在有一百五十年。這是現在世界中頭

United States of America. This state, which has now existed for one hundred fifty years, was the first in the modern world to carry out the principles of democracy. Ten years after the establishment of the American Republic, the French Revolution was precipitated. The situation at the time of the French Revolution was like this: Since Louis XIV had seized all the power of the state and exercised absolute despotism, the people of France had suffered untold miseries; when his heirs displayed an even greater cruelty and wickedness, the people were goaded beyond endurance and started to revolt. They killed Louis XVI just as the English had killed Charles I, after giving him a public trial and proclaiming his disloyalty to the state and to the people. But then all the other states of Europe arose to avenge the death of the French king and war was fought for over ten years, with the result that the revolution failed and monarchy lifted its head once more. From this time on, however, democratic ideas flourished all the more among the French people.

Everyone who discusses the history of democracy knows about the French philosopher Rousseau, who advocated popular rights in an extreme form and whose democratic theories generated the French Rev-

一個實行民權的國家。美國建立共和以後，不到十年，便引出法國革命。法國當時革命的情形，是因爲自路易十四總攬政權，厲行專制，人民受非常的痛苦。他的子孫繼位，更是暴虐無道，人民忍無可忍，於是發生革命，把路易十六殺了。法國人殺路易十六，也是和英國人殺查理士第一一樣，把他拿到法庭公開審判，宣佈他不忠於國家和人民的罪狀。法國皇帝被殺之後，歐洲各國爲他復仇，大戰十多年。所以那次的法國革命，還是失敗，帝制又恢復起來了。但是法國人民民權的思想，從此更極達發。

講到民權史，大家都知道法國有一位學者叫做盧梭，盧梭是歐洲主張極端民權的人，因有他的民權思想，便發

olution. Rousseau's most important work out of his lifelong thinking and writing upon democracy was his *Social Contract*. The idea upon which the book is built is this: Man is born with rights of freedom and equality, rights which were endowed by Nature but which he has thrown away. According to his theory, the people are given their sovereign rights by Nature; but, as we study the evolution of history, we see that democracy has not been Heaven-born but has been wrought out of the conditions of the times and the movement of events. We can find no facts in the evolution of the race to bear out Rousseau's philosophy, which, consequently, lacks foundation. Opponents of democracy take Rousseau's unfounded arguments as material for their case, but we who believe in democracy do not need to start with discussion about it; universal principles are all based first upon fact and then upon theory, theory does not precede fact.

The theory in Rousseau's *Social Contract* that the rights and the powers of the people are bestowed by Nature is fundamentally in conflict with the principle of historical evolution, and so the enemies of democracy have used Rousseau's unsound argument to stop the mouths of the supporters of democ-

生法國革命。盧梭一生民權思想最要緊的著作是民約論,民約論中立論的根據,是說人民的權利是生而自由平等的,各人都有天賦的權利,不過人民後來把天賦的權利放棄罷了。所以這種言論,可以說民權是天生出來的。但就歷史上進化的道理說,民權不是天生出來的,是時勢和潮流所造就出來的。故推到進化的歷史上,並沒有盧梭所說的那種民權事實,這就是盧梭的言論沒有根據。所以反對民權的人,便拿盧梭沒有根據的話去做材料。但是我們主張民權的,不必要先主張言論,因為宇宙間的道理,都是先有事實,然後才發生言論,並不是先有言論,然後才發生事實。

盧梭民約論中所說民權是由天賦的言論,本是和歷史上進化的道理相衝突。所以反對民權的人,便拿他那種沒有根據的言論來做口實。盧梭說民權是天賦的,本來是不合理,但是反對他的人,便拿他那

racy. Rousseau's idea that democracy is naturally endowed was unreasonable, but for opponents to use one false conclusion of his as an argument against all democracy is just as unreasonable. When we are studying the truths of the universe, we must begin by investigating the facts and not depend merely upon the treatises of scholars. Why, if Rousseau's philosophy was not based upon fact, did all the peoples welcome it? And how was Rousseau able to produce such a treatise? He saw the power of the people rising into a flood and espoused the people's sovereignty; his democratic proposals suited the psychology of the time and made the masses welcome him. So, although his theory of democracy conflicted with the principles of historical progress, the spirit of democracy which was already coming to be a reality in the life of his day caused him to be warmly received in spite of his faulty arguments. And it may be added that Rousseau's advocacy of the original idea of democracy was one of the greatest contributions to government in all history.

Since the beginning of human history, the kind of power which government has wielded has inevitably varied according to the circumstances and tendencies of the age. In an age which rev-

一句沒有根據的言論來反對民權,也是不合理。我們要研究宇宙的道理,須先要靠事實,不可專靠學者的言論。盧梭的言論,旣是沒有根據,爲甚麼當時各國還要歡迎呢?又爲甚麼盧梭能夠發生那種言論呢?因爲他當時看見民權的潮流已經湧到了,所以他便主張民權。他的民權主張,剛合當時人民的心理,所以當時的人民便歡迎他。他的言論雖然是和歷史進化的道理相衝突,但是當時的政治情形,已經有了那種事實,因爲有了那種事實,所以他引證錯誤了的言論,還是被人歡迎。至於說到盧梭提倡民權的始意,更是政治上千古的大功勞。

世界上自有歷史以來,政治上所用的權,因爲各代時勢的潮流不同,便各有不得不然的區別。比方在神權時代,非用神權不可,在君

erenced gods, theocratic power had to be used; in an age of princes autocratic power had to be used. But now the currents of the world's life have swept into the age of democracy and it behooves us quickly to study what democracy means. Because some of the treatises upon democracy, such as Rousseau's *Social Contract,* have been a bit inconsistent with true principles, is no reason why we should oppose all that is good in democracy as well. Nor must we think that democracy is impracticable because the monarchy was restored after Cromwell's revolution in England or because the revolution stretched out for so long a time in France. The French Revolution lasted eighty years before it succeeded. The American Revolution accomplished its aims in eight years, but England after two hundred years of revolution still has a king. However, if we observe the steady progress of the world from many angles, we are assured that the day of democracy is here; and that, no matter what disappointments and defeats democracy may meet, it will maintain itself for a long time to come upon the earth.

Thirty years ago, therefore, we fellow revolutionists firmly resolved that, if we wanted China to be strong and our revolution to be

權時代，非用君權不可。現在世界潮流到了民權時代，我們應該要趕快去研究，不可因為前人所發表民權的言論稍有不合理，像盧梭的民約論一樣，便連民權的好意也要反對。也不可因為英國有格林威爾革命之後，仍要復辟，和法國的革命延長，便以為民權不能實行。法國革命經過了八十年才能夠成功。美國革命不過八年，便大功告成。英國革命經過了二百多年，至今還有皇帝。但是就種種方面來觀察，世界一天進步一天，我們便知道現在的潮流，已經到了民權時代。將來無論是怎麼樣挫折，怎麼樣失敗，民權在世界上，總是可以維持長久的。

所以在三十年前，我們革命同志便下了這個決心，主張要中國強盛，實行革命，便非提

effective, we must espouse the cause of democracy. Those Chinese who opposed democracy used to ask what strength there was in our Revolutionary Party to be able to overthrow the Manchu emperor. But in 1911 he fell with one push, another victim of the world tide. This world tendency has flowed from theocracy on to autocracy and from autocracy now on to democracy, and there is no way to stem the current. Autocracy in Europe is on the wane. Great Britain uses a political party rather than a king to govern the country; it may be called a republic with a king. From all this we see that not only theocracy but also autocracy will soon crumble before the on-flowing world current. The present age of democracy is a sequence of the democratic ideas in the Greek and Roman age and, while it has been only one hundred fifty years since the beginnings of democracy, its future will be growing brighter day by day.

So we in our revolution have chosen democracy, first, that we may be following the world current, and second, that we may reduce the period of civil war. From ancient times in China, men of great ambition have all wanted to be king. Thus, when Liu Pang* saw Ch'in

倡民權不可。中國人從前反對民權，常常問我們革命黨有甚麼力量，可以推翻滿清皇帝呢？但是滿清皇帝，在辛亥年一推就倒了，這就是世界潮流的效果。世界潮流的趨勢，由神權流到君權，由君權流到民權，現在流到了民權，便沒有方法可以反抗。我們主張民權，就是順應世界的潮流。現在歐洲的君權也逐漸減少，比如英國是用政黨治國，不是用皇帝治國，可以說是有皇帝的共和國。由此可見世界潮流，到了現在，不但是神權不能夠存在，就是君權也不能夠長久。現在之民權時代，是繼續希臘羅馬之民權思想而來。自民權復興以至於今日，不過一百五十年，但是以後的時期長遠，天天應該要發達。

所以我們在中國革命，決定採用民權制度，一則為順應世界之潮流，二則為縮短國內之戰爭。因為自古以來，有大志之人，多想做皇帝，如劉邦見秦皇出外，便曰：「大丈夫當如

---

* The founder of the Han dynasty. (204 B.C.-219 A.D.)

19

Shih Hwang riding out, he said, "That is the way for men of valor!" and Hsiang Hu* also said, "Let me usurp his place!" From one generation to another, there has been no end to this unscrupulous greed for power. When I launched the revolution, six or seven out of every ten who came to our support had imperialistic ideas, but after we made it known that our revolutionary principles aimed not only at the overthrow of the Manchus but also at the establishment of a republic, this group gradually got rid of their selfish ambitions. But there are still a few among them who, even in this thirteenth year of the Republic, cling to the old hope of becoming king, and this is the reason why even among our followers there were some who fought against each other. When we first proclaimed our revolution, we lifted up the rights of the people as the basis upon which to build our republic, with the hope that this would prevent the rivalry for imperial power.

To-day I am speaking about the people's sovereignty and I want you all to understand clearly what it really means. Unless we do understand clearly, we can never get rid of imperial ambitions among us, ambitions which will make even brethren in a cause and citizens of

* A rival of Liu Pang.

20

是也」項羽亦曰：「彼可取而代也」。此等野心家代代不絕，當我提倡革命之初，其來贊成者，十人之中，差不多有六七人，是有一種皇帝思想的。但是我們宣傳革命主義，不但是要推翻滿清，並且要建設共和，所以十中之六七人，都逐漸化除其皇帝思想了。但是其中仍有一二人，就是到了民國十三年，那種做皇帝的舊思想，還沒有化除，所以跟我來做革命黨的人，也有自相殘殺，即此故也。我們革命黨於宣傳之始，便揭出民權主義來建設共和國家，就是思想免了爭皇帝之戰爭。

我現在講民權主義，便要大家明白民權究竟是甚麼意思，如果不明白這個意思，想做皇帝的心理便永遠不能消滅。大家若是有了想做皇帝的心理，一來同志就要打同志，二來本國

the same country fight one another. The whole land will be torn year after year with civil strige and there will be no end to the sufferings of the people. Because I wanted us to avert such calamities, I lifted up the banner of democracy as soon as the revolution began and determined that we should found a republic. When we have a real republic, who will be king? The people, our four hundred millions, will be king. This will prevent everybody from struggling for power and will reduce the war evil in China. The history of China shows that every change of dynasty has meant war. A peaceful period has always been followed by disorder, disorder over the rivalry for kingship. Foreign countries have had wars over religion and wars over freedom, but China in her thousands of years has had but one kind of war, the war for the throne. In order to avert further civil war, we, as soon as we launched our revolution, proclaimed that we wanted a republic and not kings.

人更要打本國人。全國長年相爭相打,人民的禍害,便沒有止境。我從前因為要免去這種禍害,所以發起革命的時候,便主張民權,決心建立一個共和國。共和國家成立以後,是用誰來做皇帝呢?是用人民來做皇帝,用四萬萬人來做皇帝。照這樣辦法,便免得大家相爭,便可以減少中國的戰禍。就中國歷史講,每換一個朝代,都有戰爭。中國歷史常是一治一亂,當亂的時候,總是爭皇帝,外國嘗有因宗教而戰自由而戰的,但中國幾千年以來,所戰的都是皇帝一個問題。我們革命黨為免將來戰爭起見,所以當初發起的時候,便主張共和,不要皇帝。

# LECTURE TWO*

## 第 二 講

民國十三年三月十六日講

FOREIGN scholars always associate "democracy" with "liberty" and many foreign books and essays discuss the two side by side. The peoples of Europe and America have warred and struggled for little else besides liberty these past two or three hundred years and, as a result, democracy is beginning to florish. The watchword of the French Revolution was "Liberty, Equality, Fraternity," just as the watchword of our Revolution is *"Min-ts'u, Min-ch'uan, Min-sheng"* (People's Nationalism, People's Sovereignty, People's Livelihood). We may say that liberty, equality, and fraternity are based upon the people's sovereignty or that the people's sovereignty develops out of liberty, equality, and fraternity. While we are discussing democracy we must consider the meaning of the French watch-word.

As revolutionary ideas have spread through the East, the word "liberty" has come too; many devoted students and supporters of the new

民權這個名詞，外國學者每每把他和自由那個名詞並稱，所以在外國很多的書本或言論裏頭，都是民權和自由並列。歐美兩三百年來，人民所奮鬪的所競爭的，沒有別的東西，就是爲自由，所以民權便由此發達。法國革命的時候，他們革命的口號，是自由、平等、博愛三個名詞。好比中國革命，用民族、民權、民生三個主義一樣。由此可說自由、平等、博愛是根據於民權，民權又是由於這三個名詞然後才發達。所以我們要講民權，便不能不先講自由、平等、博愛這三個名詞。

近來革命思潮傳到東方之後，自由這個名詞也傳進來了。許多學者志士提倡新思潮的，

* Delivered on March 16, 1924.

22

movement have sought to explain in detail its meaning, as something of vital importance. The movement for liberty has played a large part in the history of Europe the past two or three hundred years, and most European wars have been fought for liberty. So Western scholars look upon liberty as a most significant thing, and many peoples in the West have engaged in a rewarding study of its meaning. But since the word has been brought to China, only a few of the intelligentsia have had time to study and to understand it. If we should talk to the common people of China in the villages or on the streets about "liberty," they would have no idea of what we meant. So we may say that the Chinese have not gotten anything yet out of the word: even the new youth and the returned students, those who have paid some attention to Western political affairs and those who have constantly heard "liberty" talked about or have seen the word in books, have a very hazy conception of what it signifies. No wonder that foreigners criticize the Chinese, saying that their civilization is inferior and their thinking immature, that they even have no idea of liberty and no word with which to express the idea, yet at the same time critizing the Chinese for

把自由講到很詳細，視為很重要。這種思潮，在歐洲兩三百年以前，佔很重要的地位。因為歐洲兩三百年來的戰爭，差不多都是為爭自由，所以歐美學者對於自由看得很重要，一般人民對於自由的意義也很有心得。但是這個名詞近來傳進中國。祇有一般學者曾用工夫去研究過的，才懂得甚麼叫做自由。至於普通民眾，像在鄉村或街道上的人，如果我們對他們說自由，他們一定不懂得。所以中國人對於自由兩個字實在是完全沒有心得，因為這個名詞傳到中國不久。現在懂得的，不過是一般新青年和留學生，或者是留心歐美政治時務的人，常常聽到和在書本上看見這兩個字，但是究竟甚麼是自由，他們還是莫名其妙。所以外國人批評中國人，說中國人的文明程度真是太低，思想太幼稚，連自由的知識都沒有，自由的名詞都沒有。但是外國人，一面既批評中國人沒有自由的知識，一面又批評中國人是一片散沙。

being disunited as a sheet of loose sand.

These two criticisms are absolutely contradictory. What do foreigners mean when they say that China is a sheet of loose sand? Simply that every person does as he pleases and has let his individual liberty extend to all phases of life, hence China is but a lot of separate sand particles. Take up a handful of sand; no matter how much there is, the particles will slip about without any tendency to cohere—that is loose sand. But if we add cement to the loose sand, it will harden into a firm body like a rock, in which the sand, however, has no freedom. When we compare sand and rock, we clearly see that rock was originally composed of particles of sand; but in the firm body of the rock the sand has lost its power to move about freely. Liberty, to put it simply, means the freedom to move about as one wishes within an organized group. Because China does not have a word to convey this idea, everyone has been at a loss to appreciate it. We have a phrase that suggests liberty—"running wild without bridle," but that is the same thing as "loose sand"—excessive liberty for the individual. So foreigners who criti-

24

外國人的這兩種批評，在一方面說中國人是一片散沙，沒有團體。又在一方面說中國人不明白自由。這兩種批評，恰恰是相反的。為甚麼是相反的呢？比方外國人說中國人是一片散沙，究竟一片散沙的意思是甚麼呢？就是個個有自由，和人人有自由，人人把自己的自由擴充到很大，所以成了一片散沙。甚麼是一片散沙呢？如果我們拿一手沙起來，無論多少，各顆沙都是很活動的，沒有束縛的，這便是一片散沙。如果在散沙內參加士敏士，便結成石頭，變為一個堅固的團體，變成了石頭，團體很堅固，散沙便沒有自由，所以拿散沙和石頭比較，馬上就明白。石頭本是由散沙結合而成的，但是散沙在石頭的堅固團體之內，就不能活動，就失却自由。自由的解釋，簡單言之，在一個團體中，能够活動，來往自如，便是自由。因為中國沒有這個名詞，所以大家都莫名其妙。但是我們有一種固有名詞，是和自由相彷彿的，就是放蕩不羈一句話。既然是放蕩不羈，就是和散沙一樣，

cize us, who say on the one hand that we have no power to unite, are loose sand and free particles, and say on the other hand that we do not understand the meaning of "liberty"—do they not realize that it is everybody's liberty which is making us a sheet of loose sand and that if all are united in a strong body we cannot be like loose sand? These critics are "holding their spear against their own shield."

Within the last two or three centuries, foreign countries have expended enormous energy in the struggle for liberty. Is liberty really a good thing? What is it? I don't think the common people of China have the least conception of what this "liberty," that the Westerners say they have been fighting for, means. In their wars, Westerners extolled liberty to the skies and made it sacred; they even made a saying like "Give me liberty or give me death" their battle cry. Chinese students, in translating Western theories, have introduced these words into China; they have upheld liberty and determined to fight for it. In their first enthusiasm they almost equaled the Westerners in days past. But the mass of the people in China do not understand what liberty means; you must realize that liberty develops as the

各個有很大的自由。所以外國人批評中國人，一面說沒有結合能力，旣然如此，當然是散沙，是很自由的。又一面說中國人不懂自由，殊不知大家都有自由，便是一片散沙，要大家結合成一個堅固團體，便不能像一片散沙。所以外國人這樣批評我們的地方，就是陷於自相矛盾了。

最近二三百年以來，外國用了很大的力量爭自由，究竟自由是好不好呢？到底是一個甚麼東西呢？依我看來，近來兩三百年，外國人說爲自由去戰爭，我中國普通人，也總莫名其妙。他們當爭自由的時候，鼓吹自由主義，說得很神聖，甚至把「不自由毋寧死」的一句話，成了爭自由的口號。中國學者翻譯外國人的學說，也把這句話搬進到中國來，並且擁護自由，決心去奮鬥，當初的勇氣，差不多和外國人從前是一樣。但是中國一般民衆，還是不能領會甚麼是叫做自由。大家要知道自由和民權是同時發達的，所以今天來講民權，便不能不

power of the people develops. So in speaking about democracy to-day, I cannot but first speak of liberty. We must understand that Europe and America have shed much blood and have spent much life in the struggle for liberty. Democracy has been in existence for over a century in the West, but, historically, it followed the fight for liberty. Life was first poured out in order to attain liberty; the fruit of liberty was democracy. In those days the educated leaders of Europe and America held up liberty as their banner just as we in our revolution are holding up the Three Principles of the People. From all this we can see that the Western wars were first for liberty and when liberty was attained the results were called by scholars democracy. The term "democracy" comes from an old Greek word. Even now Western-ers are not very much interested in the term "democracy" and think of it more or less as a technical term in political science; it is far from being the matter of life and death which liberty has been.

But in the modern wars of Europe, liberty rather than democracy has been the aim proclaimed. Liberty was a word that everybody in Europe could easily understand. The Europeans' response to the word "liberty" is similar to the

講自由。我們要知道歐美為爭自由，流了多少血，犧牲了許多性命。歐美發生民權，已經有了一百多年，推到民權的來歷，由於爭自由之後才有的。最初歐美人民犧牲性命，本來是為爭自由，爭自由的結果，才得到民權。當時歐美學者提倡自由去戰爭，好比我們革命提倡民族、民權、民生三主義的道理是一樣的。由此可見歐美人民最初的戰爭是為自由，自由爭得之後，學者才稱這種結果為民權。所謂「德謨克拉西」，此乃希臘之古名詞，而歐美民眾至今對這個名詞亦不大關心，不過視為政治學中之一句術語便了。比之自由二字，視為性命所關，則相差遠了。

歐洲一二百多年以來的戰爭，不是說爭民權，是說爭自由，提起自由兩個字，全歐洲人便容易明白。當時歐洲人民聽了自由這個名詞容易明白的情形，好像

Chinese response to-day to the word "make a fortune" which is thought so much of in China. Liberty has been the rallying cry in modern European wars because Europeans understood the word and were willing to contend for it and to sacrifice for it; everyone worshiped liberty. Why have Europeans so cherished this word?

The people of the West sought liberty because of the extremes to which autocracy had developed. They were in a stage of civilization corresponding to the close of the Chou dynasty and the period of the coordinated states in China, about the time of the Roman Empire. Contemporaneously with the Chou, Ch'in, and Han dynasties, Rome was unifying Europe. Rome at first established a republic, but later became a monarchy. After the downfall of the Roman Empire several states sprang up simultaneously in Europe, just as the break-up of the Chou dynasty was followed by the coordinated states. So many scholars have compared the conflict of the "Seven Leaders" at the end of the Chou dynasty with the situation after the fall of Rome. After the Roman Empire had broken up into small states, the feudal system came into existence: the strongest leaders became kings and princes; the next in power, marquises; the

中國人聽了發財這個名詞一樣。歐洲當時戰爭所用的標題是爭自由，因為他們極明白這個名詞，所以人民便為自由去奮鬥，為自由去犧牲，大家便很崇拜自由。何以歐洲人民聽道自由，便那樣歡迎呢？

因為當時歐洲的君主專制發達到了極點。歐洲的文明，和中國周末列國相同，中國周末的時候，是和歐洲羅馬同時，羅馬統一歐洲，正在中國周、秦、漢的時代。羅馬初時建立共和，後來變成帝制。羅馬亡了之後，歐洲列國並峙，和中國周朝亡了之後，變成東周列國一樣，學者把周朝亡後的七雄爭長，和羅馬亡後變成列國的情形，相提並論。羅馬變成列國，成了封建制度，那個時候，大者王，小者侯，最小者還有伯子男，都是很專制的。那種封建政體，比較中國周朝的列國封建制度，還要專制得多。歐洲人民在那種專制政體之下所受的痛苦，我們今日還多想不到。比之中國歷朝人

least powerful, earls, viscounts, and barons. They all held autocratic power and the whole system of government was far more despotic than the feudal regime during the Chou dynasty in China. We to-day cannot imagine what the people of Europe suffered under their feudal rule; it was far worse than anything Chinese have ever suffered under their autocracies. The reason is this: the Ch'in dynasty* in imposing its autocracy directly on the people would make a human sacrifice of any who spoke evil of the government and execute two people for even talking together; soon afterwards the dynasty rushed headlong into ruin. So the dynasties and governments which followed the Ch'in adopted a much more liberal policy towards the people; apart from paying the regular grain taxes the people had almost no relation with the officials. The European tyranny in one way and another pressed directly down upon the shoulders of the common people. As this lasted very long and despotism developed more and more systematically, conditions became worse than anything we have ever experienced in China. So Europeans two hundred years ago were groaning under the painful yoke of autocracy just as Chinese to-day

* 246-207 B.C.

民所受專制的痛苦，還要更利害。這個原故，由於中國自秦朝專制，直接對於人民「誹謗者滅族，偶語者棄市」，遂至促亡。以後歷朝政治，大多對人民取寬大態度，人民納了糧之外，幾乎與官吏沒有關係，歐洲的專制，却一一直接專制到人民，時間復長，方法日密，那專制的進步，實在比中國利害得多。所以歐洲人在二百年以前，受那種極殘酷專制的痛苦，好像現在中國人受貧窮的痛苦是一樣。人民受久了那樣殘酷的專制，深感不自由的痛苦，所以他們唯一的方法，就是要奮鬥去爭自由，解除那種痛苦，一聽到有人說自由便很歡迎。

are groaning under the yoke of poverty. Europeans, after such a long period of cruel tyranny, felt keenly the distress which the lack of liberty brought; the only way for them to get rid of their misery was, therefore, to fight for liberty, and when men spoke of liberty they joyfully responded.

After the destruction of China's ancient feudal system, the stately pomp of autocracy hardly affected the common people. Since the Ch'in dynasty, the aim of China's emperors has been first to protect their own throne that they might continue to keep the empire in their own family and that their heirs might reign in peace forever. So any activities of the people which seemed to endanger the throne were repressed as strongly as possible. So ever since the Ch'in dynasty, succeeding emperors have cared only for their own royal power and but little about the lives of the people. As for the happiness of the people, that was not in their thoughts at all. The people had little direct relation to the emperor beyond paying him the annual grain tax—nothing more. Consequently, the political consciousness of the people has been very weak. The people did not care who was emperor. As soon as they had paid their grain tax they considered their

中國古代封建制度破壞之後，專制淫威，不能達到普通人民。由秦以後，歷代皇帝專制的目的，第一是要保守他們自己的皇位，永遠家天下，使他們子子孫孫可以萬世安享。所以對於人民的行動，於皇位有危險的，便用很大的力量去懲治，所以中國自秦以後，歷代的皇帝都祇顧皇位，並不理民事，說到人民的幸福，更是理不到。人民對於皇帝祇有一個關係，就是納糧，除了納糧之外，便和政府沒有別的關係。因爲這個原故，中國人民的政治思想，便很薄弱，人民不管誰來做皇帝，祇要納糧，便算盡了人民的責任。政府祇要人民納糧，便不去理會他們別的事，其餘都是聽人民自生自滅。由此可見中國人民

29

duty as citizens done. The emperors wanted only the grain tax from the people and were not interested in anything else they did, letting them live and die to themselves. We can see from this that the Chinese people have not been directly subject to the oppression of autocracy; their sufferings have come indirectly. Because our state has been weak, we have come under the political and economic domination of foreign countries and have not been able to resist. Now our wealth is exhausted and our people are destitute, suffering poverty because of an indirect tyranny.

The Chinese people, therefore, felt very little resentment against their emperors. On the other hand, the autocracy of Europe was quite different from that of China. The despotism in Europe, from the downfall of Rome up to two or three centuries ago, had been developing rapidly and the people had suffered increasingly and unbearably. Many kinds of liberty were denied them, chiefly liberty of thought, liberty of speech, and liberty of movement. Take freedom of belief. When people who live in a certain place are forced to believe in a particular religion, whether they want to or not, the situation becomes very hard to bear. Europeans indeed suffered "deep

直接並沒有受過很大的專制痛苦,只有受間接的痛苦。因為國家衰弱,受外國政治經濟的壓迫沒有力量抵抗,弄到民窮財盡;人們便受貧窮的痛苦,這種痛苦,就是間接的痛苦,不是直接的痛苦。

所以當時人民對於皇帝的怨恨還是少的。但是歐洲的專制,就和中國的不同,歐洲由羅馬亡後到兩三百年以前,君主的專制是很進步的,所以人民所受的痛苦,也是很利害的,人民是很難忍受的。當時人民受那種痛苦,不自由的地方極多,最大的是思想不自由,言論不自由,行動不自由。譬如就信仰不自由說,人民在一個甚麼地方住,便強迫要信仰一種甚麼宗教,不管人民是情願不情願,由此人民都很難忍受。歐洲人民當時

waters and burning fires" from the denial of freedom. So, whenever they heard of anyone leading a struggle for liberty, they all rejoiced and espoused his cause. Such was the beginning of the European revolutionary idea.

There is a deep significance in the proposal of our Revolutionary Party that the Three Principles of the People, rather than a struggle for liberty, should be the basis of our revolution. The watchword of the French Revolution was "Liberty"; the watchword of the American Revolution was "Independence"; the watchword of our Revolution is the "Three Principles of the People." We spent much time and effort before we decided upon our watchword; we are not merely imitating others. The peoples of Europe suffered so bitterly from despotism that as soon as the banner of liberty was lifted high, millions with one heart rallied about it. If we in China, where the people have not suffered such despotism, should make the cry of liberty, no attention would be paid to it.

Modern European scholars who observe China all say that our civilization is so backward and our political consciousness so weak that we do not even understand liberty. "We Europeans," they declare, "fought and sacrificed for liberty

受那種種不自由的痛苦，真是水深火熱，所以一聽到說有人提倡爭自由，大家便極歡迎，便去附和，這就是歐洲革命思潮的起源。

我們革命黨向來主張三民主義去革命，而不主張以革命去爭自由，是很有深意的。從前法國革命的口號是自由，美國革命的口號是獨立，我們革命的口號就是三民主義。是用了很多時間，做了很多工夫，才定出來的，不是人云亦云。歐洲人民因為從前受專制的痛苦太深，所以一經提倡自由，便萬衆一心去贊成。假若現在中國來提倡自由，人民向來沒有受過這種痛苦，當然不理會。

近來歐洲學者觀察中國，每每說中國的文明程度太低，政治思想太薄弱，連自由都不懂，我們歐洲人在一二百年前為自由戰爭，為自由犧牲，不知道做了多

31

one or two hundred years ago and performed no one knows how many startling deeds, but Chinese still do not know what liberty is. This shows that the political thinking of us Europeans is far superior to the political thinking of the Chinese." Because we do not talk about liberty, they say that we are poor in political ideas. I don't think such an argument gets anywhere. If Europeans value liberty so much, why do they call the Chinese a "sheet of loose sand"? When Europeans were struggling for liberty, they naturally took a strong view of liberty, but since they have won liberty and have reached their goal, their conception of liberty has probably become weaker. If the banner of liberty should be raised again to-day, I don't think it would call forth the same enthusiasm as before. Moreover, struggles for liberty was the European method of revolution two or three centuries ago and could not be repeated now. To use the figure "loose sand," what is its chief characteristic?—Its absolute freedom, without which there can be no such thing as loose sand. When European democracy was just budding, Europeans talked about fighting for liberty; when they had gained their end, everyone began to extend the limits of his individual liberty and soon the ex-

少驚天動地的事，現在中國人還不懂自由是甚麼，由此便可見我們歐洲人的政治思想，比較中國人高得多。由於中國人不講自由，便說是政治思想薄弱，這種言論，依我看起來，是講不通的。因為歐洲人旣看重自由，為甚麼又說中國人是一片散沙呢？歐洲人從前要爭自由的時候，他們自由的觀念自然是很濃厚，得到了自由之後，目的已達，恐怕他們的自由觀念，也漸漸淡薄。如果現在再去提倡自由，我想一定不像從前那樣的歡迎。而且歐洲爭自由的革命，是兩三百年前的舊方法，一定是做不通的。就一片散沙而論，有甚麼精采呢？精采就是在有充分的自由，如果不自由，便不能够成一片散沙。從前歐洲在民權初萌芽的時代，便主張爭自由，到了目的已達，各人都擴充自己的自由，於是由於自由太過，便發生了許多流弊。所以英國有一個學者叫做彌勒氏的，便說一個人的自由，以不侵犯他人的自由為範圍，才

cesses of liberty led to many evil consequences. Therefore an English scholar named Mill* said that only individual liberty which did not interfere with the liberty of others can be considered true liberty. If one's liberty is incompatible with another's sphere of liberty, it is no longer liberty. Before that, Westerners had set no limits upon freedom, but when Mill proposed his theory of a limited freedom, the measure of personal liberty was considerably reduced. Evidently Western scholars had come to realize that liberty was not a sacred thing which could not be encroached upon, but that it must be put within boundaries.

When we think about that "sheet of loose sand" we realize that the Chinese have had a great measure of liberty. Because Chinese have had an excessive degree of liberty, they have given it no concern, just as when there is plenty of fresh air in the room we do not realize its value; but when the doors and the windows are closed and no fresh air can come in, we know its importance. Europeans under the despotism of two or three centuries ago had no liberty whatsoever, so every man appreciated how precious a thing liberty was and was ready to

* Referring to John Stuart Mill.

是真自由。如果侵犯他人的範圍，便不是自由。歐美人講自由，從前沒有範圍，到英國彌勒氏才立了自由的範圍，有了範圍，便減少很多自由了。由此可知彼中學者，已漸知自由不是一個神聖不可侵犯之物，所以也要定一個範圍來限制他了。

我們拿一片散沙的事實來研究，便知道中國人有很多的自由，因為自由太多，故大家便不注意去理會，連這個名詞也不管了。中國人因為自由過於充分，便不去理會。好比房中的空氣太多，我們便不覺得空氣有甚麼重要，到了關閉門戶，沒有空氣進來，我們才覺得空氣是個很重要的。歐洲人在兩三百年以前受專制的痛苦，完全沒有自由，所以他們人人才知道自由可貴，要拚命去爭

33

give his life for it. Before they won liberty, they were like men shut up in a small room; after they had won liberty they were like men suddenly let out into the open air. Naturally everyone felt that liberty was something of wonderful value and was saying, "Give me liberty or give me death."

Europeans and Americans risked their lives in the battles for liberty a hundred and fifty years ago, because liberty was rare for them. When nations like France and the United States won liberty, they became what we call the pioneers in democratic government. Yet even in these two countries, is everyone free? The liberty which Westerners talk about has its strict limitations and cannot be described as belonging to everyone. Young Chinese students when they talk about liberty break down all restraints. Because no one welcomes their theory in the society outside, they can only bring it back into their own schools, and constant disorders and strikes result. This is abuse of freedom. That foreigners should not be familiar with Chinese history and should not know that since ancient times Chinese have enjoyed a large measure of liberty, is not strange. But that our own students should have forgotten the Liberty

。沒有爭到自由之先，好像是閉在小房裏一樣，既爭到了自由之後，好比是從小房內忽然放出來，遇着了空氣一樣。所以大家便覺得自由是很貴重的東西，所以他們常常說「不自由毋寧死」那一句話。

歐美人在一百五十年以前，因為難得自由，所以拚命去爭，既爭到了之後，像法國、美國，是我們所稱為實行民權先進的國家，在這兩個國家之內，人人是不是都有自由呢？歐美人講自由，是有很嚴格界限的，不能說人人都有自由。中國新學生講自由，把甚麼界限都打破了。拿這種學說到外面社會，因為沒有人歡迎，所以只好搬回學校內去用，故常常生出鬧學風潮，此自由之用之不得其所也。外國人不識中國歷史，不知道中國人民自古以來都有很充分的自由，這自是難怪。至於中國的學生，而竟忘卻了「日出而作，日入而息，鑿井而飲，耕田而食，帝力於我何有哉？」這個先民的

Song of the ancient Chinese—
*"When the sun rises, I toil;*
*When the sun sets, I rest;*
*I dig wells for water;*
*I till the fields for food;*
*What has the Emperor's power*
*to do with me?"*
is surprisingly strange. We can see
from this Liberty Song that China,
while she has not had liberty in
name, has had liberty in fact from
days of old, and so much of it that
she need not seek for more.

If foreigners say that we are a
sheet of loose sand, we will acknowledge the truth, but we cannot ac-
cept their assertion that the Chinese
have no understanding of liberty
and are weak in their political consciousness. Why has China become a sheet of loose sand? Simply
because of excessive individual
liberty. Therefore the aims of the
Chinese Revolution are different
from the aims in foreign revolutions,
and the methods we use must also
be different. Why, indeed, is
China having a revolution? To put
the answer directly, the aims of our
revolution are just opposite to the
aims of the revolutions of Europe.
Europeans rebelled and fought for
liberty because they had had too
little liberty. But we, because we
have had too much liberty without
any unity and resisting power, because we have become a sheet of

自由歌，却是大可怪的
事。由這個自由歌看起
來，便知中國自古以來
，雖無自由之名，而確
有自由之實，且極其充
分，不必再去多求了。

所以外國人說中國
人是一片散沙，我們是
承認的，但是說中國人
不懂自由，政治思想薄
弱，我們便不能承認。
中國人爲甚麼是一片散
沙呢？由於甚麼東西弄
成一片散沙呢？就是因
爲是各人的自由太多。
由於中國人自由太多，
所以中國要革命。中國
革命的目的與外國不同
，所以方法也不同。到
底中國爲甚麼要革命呢
？直截了當說，是和歐
洲革命的目的相反。歐
洲從前因爲太沒有自由
，所以革命要去爭自由
。我們是因爲自由太多
，沒有團體，沒有抵抗
力，成一片散沙。因爲
是一片散沙，所以受外
國帝國主義的侵略，受

loose sand and so have been invaded by foreign imperialism and oppressed by the economic control and trade wars of the Powers, without being able to resist, must break down individual liberty and become pressed together into an unyielding body like the firm rock which is formed by the addition of cement to sand.

Western revolutions began with the struggle for liberty; only after war and agitation of two or three centuries was the liberty realized from which democracy sprang. The watchword of the French Revolution was "Liberty, Equality, Fraternity." Our watchword is "People's Nationalism, People's Sovereignty, People's Livelihood." What relation do the two watchwords have to each other? According to my interpretation, our Nationalism may be said to correspond to their Liberty, because putting the People's Nationalism into effect means a struggle for the liberty of our nation. The Europeans fought for individual liberty, but to-day we have a different use for liberty. Now how shall the term "liberty" be applied? If we apply it to a person, we shall become a sheet of loose sand; on no account must we give more liberty to the individual; let us secure liberty instead for the nation. The

列強經濟商戰的壓迫，我們現在便不能抵抗。要將來能夠抵抗外國的壓迫，就要打破各人的自由。結成很堅固的團體，像把士敏土參加到散沙裏頭，結成一塊堅固石頭一樣。

外國革命，是由爭自由而起，奮鬥了兩三百年，生出了大風潮，才得到自由，才發生民權。從前法國革命的口號，是用自由、平等、博愛。我們革命的口號，是用民族、民權、民生。究竟我們三民主義的口號，和自由、平等、博愛三個口號，有甚麼關係呢？照我講起來，我們的民族，可以說和他們的自由一樣，因為實行民族主義，就是為國家爭自由。但歐洲當時是為個人爭自由，到了今天，自由的用法便不同。在今天自由這個名詞究竟要怎麼樣應用呢？如果用到個人，就成一片散沙，萬不可再用到個人上去，要用到國家上去，個人不可太過自由，國家要得完全自由。到了國家能夠

individual should not have too much liberty, but the nation should have complete liberty. When the nation can act freely, then China may be called strong. To make the nation free, we must each sacrifice his personal freedom. Students who sacrifice their personal liberty will be able to work diligently day after day and spend time and effort upon learning; when their studies are completed, their knowledge is enlarged and their powers have multiplied, then they can do things for the nation. Soldiers who socrifice their personal liberty will be able to obey orders, repay their country with loyalty and help the nation to attain liberty. If students and soldiers talk liberty, they will soon have "unrestrained license," to use a Chinese Phrase for liberty. Schools will have no rules and the army will have no discipline. How can you have a school without rules? What kind of army is that without discipline?

Why do we want the nation to be free?—Because China under the domination of the Powers has lost her national standing. She is not merely a semi-colony; she has indeed become a hypo-colony. If we want to restore China's liberty, we must unite ourselves into one unshakable body; we must use rev-

行動自由，中國便是強盛的國家。要這樣做去，便要大家犧牲自由。當學生的能夠犧牲自由，就可以天天用功，在學問上做工夫。學問成了，智識發達，能力豐富，便可以替國家做事。當軍人能夠犧牲自由，就能服從命令，忠心報國，使國家有自由。如果學生軍人要講自由，便像中國自由的對待名詞，成為放任放蕩，在學校內便沒有校規，在軍隊內便沒有軍紀。在學校內不講校規，在軍隊內不講軍紀，那麼能夠成為學校號稱軍隊嗎？

我們為甚麼要國家自由呢？因為中國受列強的壓迫，失去了國家的地位，不祇是半殖民地，實在已成了次殖民地，所以現在的國家，是很不自由的。要把我們國家的自由恢復起來，就要集合自由成一個很堅固的團體，要用革

olutionary methods to weld our state into firm unity. Without revolutionary principles we shall never succeed. Our revolutionary principles are the cement. If we can consolidate our four hundred millions and form a mighty union and make the union free, the Chinese state will be free and the Chinese people will be really free. Compare the watchword of the French Revolution with that of ours. "Liberty" in the French revolutionary watchword and "People's Nationalism" in our watchword are similar. The People's Nationalism calls for the freedom of our nation. "Equality" is similar to our "Principle of the People's Sovereignty which aims to destroy autocracy and make all men equal. "Fraternity" originally meant brothers and has the same significance as the Chinese word *t'ung-pao* (compatriots). The idea in "Fraternity" is similar to our "Principle of the People's Livelihood," which plans for the happiness of our four hundred millions.

命的方法把國家成一個大堅固團體，非有革命主義不成功。我們的革命主義，便是集合起來的士敏土，能够把四萬萬人都用革命主義集合起來，成一個大團體。這一個大團體，能够自由，中國國家當然是自由，中國民族才眞能自由。用我們三民主義的口號和法國革命的口號來比較，法國的自由和我們的民族主義相同，因爲民族主義是提倡國家自由的。平等和我們的民權主義相同，因爲民權主義是提倡人民在政治之地位都是平等的，要打破君權，使人人都是平等的，所以說民權是和平等相對待的。此外還有博愛的口號，這個名詞的原文，是兄弟的意思，和中國同胞兩個字是一樣解法，普通譯成博愛。當中的道理，和我們的民生主義是相通的。因爲我們的民生主義，是圖四萬萬人幸福的，爲四萬萬人謀幸福就是博愛。

# LECTURE THREE

## 第 三 講

MIN-CH'UAN, the People's Sovereignty is the second part of our revolutionary watchword and corresponds to equality in the French watchword. So to-day let us take equality as the theme for our study. The word "equality" is usually associated with the word "liberty." During the former revolutions in the various countries of Europe, all the people expended an almost equal amount of strength and sacrified to a similar degree in their fight for liberty and equality, and consequently they valued equality as much as they did liberty. Moreover, many people felt that if they could secure liberty, they would certainly attain to equality, and that if they did not become equal, there was no way to manifest their freedom; they regarded equality as being even higher than liberty. What is equality and whence does it come? The revolutionary philosophy of Europe and America spoke of liberty as something bestowed by Nature upon man. For example, the "Declaration of Independence" of the

民權兩個字，是我們革命黨的第二個口號，同法國革命口號的平等是相對待的。因為平等是法國革命的第二個口號，所以今天專拿平等做題目來研究。平等這名詞，通常和自由那個名詞，都是相提並論的。歐洲各國從前革命，人民為爭平等和爭自由，都是一樣的出力，一樣的犧牲，所以他們把平等和自由都是看得一樣的重大。更有許多人以為要能夠自由，必要得到平等，如果得不到平等，便無從實現自由。用平等和自由比較，把平等更是看得重大的。甚麼是叫做平等呢？平等是從那裏來的呢？歐美的革命學說，都講平等是天賦到人類的，譬如美國在革命時候

39

American Revolution and the "Declaration of the Rights of Man and of the Citizen" of the French Revolution both pronouncedly and emphatically proclaimed that liberty and equality were natural and inalienable rights of man.

Are men really born with the special right of equality? We traced the history of people's rights from the age of primitive man millions of years ago down to the beginning of our modern democratic period, but we did not discover any principle of natural human equality. In the world of Nature we do not find any two things level, except upon the surface of water. On level ground there is no place truly level. The railway runs through a natural plane; but if you look out of your coach window along the way and observe carefully the contour of the land, you will find that there is not a mile of track but has required human labor and engineering to make it level.

Nature originally did not make man equal; but when autocracy developed among mankind, the despotic kings and princes pushed human differences to an extreme, and the result was an inequality far worse than Nature's inequality. The inequality created by kings and princes was an artificial inequality.

的獨立宣言，法國在革命時候的人權宣言，都是大書特書，說平等、自由是天賦到人類的特權，人類不能侵奪的。

天生人究竟是否賦有平等的特權呢？自人類初生幾百萬年以前，推到近來民權萌芽時代，從沒有見過天賦有平等的道理。譬如用天生的萬物來講，除了水面以外，沒有一物是平的，就是拿平地來比較，也沒有一處是真平的。好像坐火車，過細考察沿路的高低情況，沒有那一里路，不是用人工修築，才可以得平路的。

天生人類本來也是不平等的，到了人類專制發達以後，專制帝王尤其變本加厲，弄到結果，比較天生的更是不平等了。這種由帝王造成的不平等，是人為的不平等。人為的不平等，究竟是甚麼情形？現在可就講壇的黑板上，

To illustrate the conditions it resulted in, let me draw a diagram on the
blackboard here:

DIAGRAM I—INEQUALITY

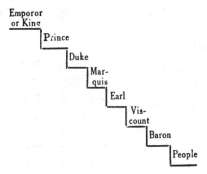

Study this diagram carefully and
you will understand what artificial
inequality meant. Because of those
artificial ranks, the specially pri-
vileged classes became excessively
cruel and iniquitous, while the
oppressed people, unable to contain
themselves, finally broke into re-
bellion and warred upon inequality.
The original aim in the revolutions
had been the destruction of man-
made inequalities; when that was
completed, men thought their revolution would be over. But the
men who occupied the high stations
of emperor and king all assumed a
divine appointment as a shield for
their office; they said that they had
received their special position from
God and that the people who opposed them would be opposing God.
The ignorant masses, who did not

繪一個圖來表明，請諸
君細看第一圖，便可明
白。

第一圖　不　平　等

因爲有這種人爲的不平
等，在特殊階級的人，
過於暴虐無道，被壓迫
的人民，無地自容，所
以發生革命的風潮，來
打不平。革命的始意，
本是在打破人爲的不平
等，到了平等以後，便
可了事。但是佔了帝王
地位的人，每每假造天
意，做他們的保障，說
他們所處的特殊地位，
是天所授與的，人民反
對他們，便是逆天，無
知識的民衆，不曉得研
究這些話，是不是合道
理，只是盲從附和，爲
君主去爭權利，來反對
有知識的人民，去講平
等自由。因此贊成革命
的學者，便不得不創天

41

study to see whether there were any truth or not in these words, followed on blindly and fought for more privileges for their kings. They even opposed the intelligent people who talked about equality and liberty. So the scholars who were supporting revolution had to invent the theory of nature-bestowed rights of equality and liberty in order to overthrow the despotism of kings. Their original purpose was to break down artificial, man-made inequalities. But in everything, certainly, "action is easy, understanding difficult"; the masses of Europe at that time believed that emperors and kings were divinely sent and had special "divine rights," and large numbers of ignorant folk supported them. No matter what methods or how much energy the small group of intelligent and educated people used, they could not overthrow the monarchs.

Finally, when the belief that man is born free and equal and that the struggle for freedom and equality is the duty of everybody had permeated the masses, the emperors and kings of Europe fell automatically. But after their downfall, the people began to believe firmly in the theory of natural equality and kept on working day after day to make all men equal. They did not know that such a thing is impossible.

賦人權的平等自由這一說，以打破君主的專制。學者創造這一說，原來就是想打破人為之不平等的。但是天下的事情，的確是行易知難，當時歐洲的民眾都相信帝王是天生的，都是受了天賦之特權的，多數無知識的人總是去擁戴他們，所以少數有知識的人們，無論用甚麼方法和力量，總是推不倒他們。

到了後來，相信天生人類都是平等自由的，爭平等自由，是人人應該有的事，然後歐洲的帝王，便一個一個不推自倒了。不過專制帝王推倒以後，民眾又深信人人是天生平等的這一說。便日日去做工夫，想達到人人的平等。殊不知這種事是不可能的。到了近來，科學昌

Only recently, in the light of science, have people begun to realize that there is no principle of natural equality. If we acted according to the belief of the masses at that time, regardless of the truth, and forced an equality upon human society, that equality would be a false one.

DIAGRAM II—FALSE EQUALITY

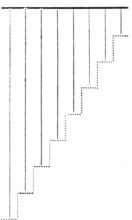

| The Sage | The Superior Man | The Genius | The Wise Man | The Average Man | The Mediocre Man | The Dullard | The Inferior Man |
|---|---|---|---|---|---|---|---|

As this second diagram shows, we would have to level down superior position in order to get equality at the top, but the line representing the standing ground of these different types would still be uneven and not level. The equality we secured would be a false equality. Equal position in human society is something to start with; each man builds up his career upon this start according to his natural endowments

明，人類大覺悟了，才知道沒有天賦平等的道理。假若照民衆相信的那一說去做，縱使不顧眞理，勉強做成功，也是一種假平等。

第二圖　假　平　等

聖　賢　才　智　平　庸　愚　劣

像第二圖一樣，必定要把位置高的壓下去。成了平頭的平等，至於立脚點還是彎曲線，還是不能平等，這種平等，不是眞平等，是假平等。說到社會上的地位平等，是始初起點的地位平等，後來各人根據天賦的聰明才力，自己去造就，因爲各人的

43

of intelligence and ability. As each man has different gifts of intelligence and ability, so the resultant careers will be different. And since each man works differently, they certainly cannot work on an equal basis. This brings us to the only true principle of equality. If we pay no attention to each man's intellectual endowments and capacities and push down those who rise to a high position in order to make all equal, the world will not progress and mankind will retrocede. When we speak of democracy and equality but yet want the world to advance, we are talking about political equality. For equality is an artificial not a natural thing, and the only equality which we can create is equality in political status.

聰明才力有天賦的不同，所以造就的結果，當然不同，造就旣是不同，自然不能有平等，像這樣講來，才是眞正平等的道理。如果不管各人天賦的聰明才力，就是以後有造就高的地位，也要把他們壓下去，一律要平等，世界便沒有進步，人類便要退化，所以我們講民權平等，又要世界有進步，是要人民在政治上的地位平等。因爲平等是人爲的，不是天生的，人造的平等，只有做到政治上的地位平等。

DIAGRAM III—TRUE EQUALITY　　　第三圖　眞平等

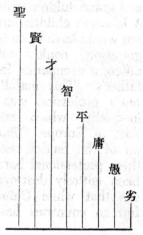

After the revolution, we want every man to have an equal political standing, such as is represented by the base line in Diagram III. This is the only true equality and true principle of nature.

The situation which existed under European despotism before the days of revolution was far more serious than the situation in China has ever been. Why was this true? —Because of the hereditary system in Europe. The European emperors, kings, princes, dukes, marquises, and other nobles passed their ranks on from generation to generation; no one ever changed from his inherited vocation. The occupations of the common people were also hereditary; they could never do anything else. If a man was a tiller of the soil, his children and grandchildren would be farmers. A laborer's children and grandchildren would have to do bitter toil. The grandson could not choose a different occupation from his grandfather's. This inability to change one's profession was the kind of inequality which existed at that time in Europe. Since the breakup of the feudal system in China, these professional barriers have also been entirely destroyed. Thus we see that while China along with foreign countries has had a class

故革命以後，必要各人在政治上的立足點都是平等，好像第三圖的底線，一律是平的，那才是眞平等，那才是自然之眞理。

歐洲沒有革命以前的情形，和中國比較起來，歐洲的專制，要比中國利害得多，原因是在甚麼地方呢？就是在世襲制度。當時歐洲的帝王公侯那些貴族，代代都是世襲貴族，不去做別種事業，人民也代代都是世襲一種事業，不能夠去做別種事業。比方耕田的人，他的子子孫孫便要做農夫，做工的人，他的子子孫孫便要做苦工。祖父做一種甚麼事業，子孫就不能改變。這種職業上不能夠改變，就是當時歐洲的不自由。中國自古代封建制度破壞以後，這種限制，也完全打破。由此可見從前中國和外國，都是有階級制度，都是不平等。中國的好處，是只有皇帝是世襲，除非有人把他推翻，才不能世襲，如果不被人推翻，代代總是世襲，到了改朝換姓，才

45

system and a kind of inequality, yet China has had the advantage, since only the emperor's rank was hereditary. Unless the emperor was overthrown, the right to reign was passed from one generation to another in the same family. Only when there was a change of dynasty did the line of emperors change. But as for dukes, marquises, earls, viscounts, and barons, these titles were changed from one generation to another even in olden days. Many commoners have become ministers of state or have been appointed princes and nobles; these were not hereditary offices. There may have been a few commoners in Europe who became ministers of state or were elevated to the nobility, but the majority of titles were hereditary and the common people were not free in choosing their occupations. This lack of freedom was what caused them to lose their equality. Not only were the political ranks not equal, but the social classes of the common people were unequal. Consequently, it was very difficult for the common people, first, to reach the position of duke, marquis, earl, viscount, or baron, and, second, to change their own occupations freely and thus rise in life. At last they came to feel that they could no longer endure the afflictions of

換皇帝。至於皇帝以下的公侯伯子男，中國古時都是可以改換的，平民做宰相封王侯的極多，不是代代世襲一種事業的。歐洲平民間或也有做宰相封王侯的。但是大多數的王侯，都是世襲，人民的職業不能自由，因為職業不自由，所以失了平等。不但是政治的階級不平等，就是人民彼此的階級也不平等。由於這個原故，人民一來難到公侯伯子男的那種地位，二來自己的職業又不自由改變，更求上進，於是感覺非常痛苦，不能忍受。所以不得不拚命去爭自由，解除職業不自由的束縛，以求上進，拚命去爭平等，打破階級專制的不平等。那種戰爭，那種奮鬥，在中國是向來沒有的。中國人雖然受過了不平等的界限，但是沒有犧牲身家性命去做平等的代價。歐洲人民在兩三百年以

this system, that they must throw their lives into a struggle for liberty, emancipate themselves from non-freedom of occupation and strive to progress. Such a war for liberty, such a demolishing of tyrannical class inequality, has never been witnessed in China. Although the Chinese have experienced class distinctions, yet they have never sacrificed their own lives or their families as a price for liberty. The revolutions of the European peoples have concentrated upon achieving liberty and equality, but the Chinese have never really understood what these things mean. The reason for this is that China's autocracy, in comparison with Europe's has not been at all severe. And although China's government was autocratic in ancient times and has not made any progress in the last two thousand years, yet before that period many reforms had been made and the abuse of despotism had been considerably reduced. Consequently, the people have not suffered very much from the autocratic system and have not fought for the principle of equality.

Since European civilization has spread its influence eastward, European political systems, economics, and science have also penetrated China. When the Chinese hear European political doctrines they

前的革命，都是集中到自由平等兩件事。中國人向來不懂甚麼是爭自由平等，當中原因，就是中國的專制和歐洲比較，實在沒有甚麼利害。而且中國古時的政治，雖然是專制，二千多年以來，雖然沒有進步，但是以前改良了很多，專制淫威也減除了不少，所以人民便不覺得十分痛苦。因為不覺得痛苦，便不為這個道理去奮鬥。

近來歐洲文化東漸，他們的政治經濟科學都傳到中國來了。中國人聽到歐洲的政治學理，多數都是照本抄謄，

generally copy them word for word without any thought of modification. The European revolutions two and three centuries ago were "struggles for liberty," so China now must struggle for liberty! Europeans fought for equality, so China must fight for equality also! But China's weakness to-day is not the lack of liberty and equality. If we try to arouse the spirit of the people with "Liberty and Equality," we will be talking wide of the point. Our people are not cut deeply enough by these things; they are not sensitive to them, and so would certainly not join our banner. But the people of Europe two or three centuries ago suffered "waters of tribulation and fires of torment" from the loss of liberty and equality; they felt that unless they could achieve liberty and equality, no question could be solved, and so they hazarded their lives in the struggle for them.

Take the United States again. The objective in the minds of the American people during their revolution was independence. Why? Because their thirteen colonies were all British territory and under British control. Great Britain was a despotic monarchy and was oppressing the American people much more severely than she oppressed her own people. When the Ameri-

全不知道改變。所以歐洲兩三百年以前的革命，說是爭自由，中國人也說要爭自由，歐洲從前爭平等，中國人也照樣要爭平等。但是中國今日的弊病，不是在不自由不平等的這些地方，如果專拿自由平等去提倡民氣，便是離事實太遠，和人民沒有切膚之痛，他們便沒有感覺，沒有感覺，一定不來附和。至於歐洲在兩三百年以前，人民所受不自由不平等的痛苦，真是水深火熱，以爲非爭到自由平等，甚麼問題都不能解決，所以拚命去爭自由打平等。

我們再拿美國來講，美國革命的時候，人民所向的目標是在獨立。他們爲甚麼要獨立呢？因爲他們當時的十三州，都是英國的領土，歸英國管理。英國是一個專制國家，壓迫美國人民，比壓迫本國人民

cans saw that they and the British were under the same government, but that British citizens were treated liberally while they themselves were so much abused, they felt keenly the inequality in the situation; they wanted to secede from Britain, govern themselves, and establish an independent state. For the sake of independence they resisted Britain and engaged in war with her for eight years until they achieved their purpose. The American government has treated its white races alike, on a basis of equality, but its treatment of colored races has been very different. The African negroes, for instance, were looked upon as slaves. Then there were many earnest people who made investigations into the sufferings of the negro slaves and published reports of what they saw. The most famous of these described many actual tragic facts of slave life in the form of a novel, which was read by everybody with intense interest. This book was called "The Black Slave's Cry to Heaven,"* and when it came out, people realized what the slaves were enduring and were indignant on their behalf. Then all the Northern States which did not use slave labor advocated the freeing of the slaves. The Southern States owned a vast num-

* Chinese title of Uncle Tom's Cabin.

還要嚴厲得多。美國人民見得他們自己和英國人民，都是同歸一個英國政府管理，英國政府待本國人民是那樣寬大，待美國人民是這樣刻薄，便覺得很不平等。所以要脫離英國，自己去管理自己，成一個獨立國家。他們因為獨立，反抗英國，和英國戰爭了八年，後來獨立成功，所有在美國的白色人種，政府都一律看待，一律平等。但是對待別色人種，便大不相同，比方在美國的非洲黑人，他們便視為奴隸，所以美國獨立之後，白人的政治地位，雖然是平等，但是黑人和白人比較，便不是平等。於是有許多熱心的人，調查當時黑奴所受的痛苦，做成了許多紀錄，其中最著名的一本書，是把黑奴受痛苦的種種事實，編成一本小說，令人看到了之後，都很有趣味，這本小說是叫做「黑奴籲天錄」。自這本書做出之後，大家都知道黑奴是怎麼樣受苦，便替黑奴來抱不平。當時全美國之中，北方

ber of slaves; each southern state had numerous vast plantations which depended solely upon slave labor for cultivation. If they should free the slaves, they would have no hard labor and could not plant their fields. The Southerners, from selfish motives, opposed emancipation, saying that the slave system was not started by one man only.

Therefore, although agitation for the freing of the slaves had begun long before, there was still a period of ferment, and it is only sixty years since the final explosion took place, precipitating the war between the North and the South. This war lasted five years, and was one of the world's great wars. It was a war against the inequality of the black slave, a war against known inequality, a war for equality.

The war resulted in defeat for the South and victory for the North, and the government of the United States immediately issued a proclamation freeing the slaves throughout the country.

The freeing of the slaves was one of the struggles for equality in American history. The two finest periods in American history were: first, when the people, suffering under the unequal treatment of the British, waged the War of Inde-

各省沒有畜黑奴的,便主張放奴。南方各省所畜的黑奴是很多的,因為南方各省有許多極大的農場,平常都是專靠黑奴去耕種,如果放黑奴,便沒有苦工,便不能耕種。南方的人由於自私自利的思想,便反對放奴,說黑奴制度不是一人起來的。

所以放黑奴的風潮,雖然是發生了很久,但是醞釀復醞釀,到了六十年前,才爆發出來,構成美國的南北戰爭。那次戰爭,兩方死了幾十萬人,打過了五年仗,雙方戰爭是非常激烈的,是世界最大戰爭之一。那次戰爭,是替黑奴打不平,替人類打不平等的,可以說是爭平等的戰爭。

那次戰爭的結果,南方打敗了,北方打勝了,聯邦政府就馬上發一個命令,要全國放奴。

解放黑奴,是美國歷史上一件爭平等的事業,所以講美國最好的歷史,第一個時期是由於受英國不平等的待遇,人民發起獨立戰爭,打過了八年仗才脫離英

pendence and, after eight years of fighting, broke away from Britain and established an independent state; second, when sixty years later the war between the North and the South was fought, for a cause similar to that of the War for Independence. The Civil War lasted five years, while the Revolutionary War lasted eight years. So American history is a story of struggle for equality and makes a shining page in the history of the world.

After the war for equality in America, a revolutionary struggle for equality broke out in France also. The conflict experienced vicissitudes over a period of eighty years before it could be counted a success. But after equality had been secured, the people pushed the word "equality" to an extreme and wanted to put everyone on the same level. It was the kind of equality which diagram II represents: the line of equality was not placed underfoot but overhead — false equality.

China's tide of revolutionary ideas came from Europe and America, and the theory of equality has also been introduced from the West. But our Revolutionary Party advocates a struggle, not for liberty and equality, but for the Three Principles of the People. If we can put these Three Principles into

國，得到平等，成一個獨立國家。第二個時期，是在六十年前，發生南北戰爭，那次戰爭的理由，和頭一次獨立戰爭是相同的，打過了五年仗。所以美國歷史是一種爭平等的歷史。這種爭平等的歷史，是世界歷史中的大光榮。

美國爭得平等之後，法國也發生革命，去爭平等。當中反覆了好幾次，爭了八十年，才算成功。但是平等爭成功之後，他們人民把平等兩個字走到極端，要無論那一種人都是平等，像第二圖所講的平等，把平等地位不放在立足點。要放在平頭點，就那是假平等。

中國的革命思潮，是發源於歐美，平等自由的學說，也是由歐美傳進來的。但是中國革命黨，不主張爭平等自由，主張爭三民主義。三民主義能夠實行，便有自由平等。歐美爲平等自由去戰爭，爭得了

practice, we will have liberty and equality. Although Western nations warred for liberty and equality, they have since been constantly led astray by them. If we put the three Principles into operation and achieve true liberty and equality, how can we be sure to keep on the right track? If, as in Diagram II, we put the line of equality at the top, we will not be following the right course. But if, as in Diagram III we make the line of equality the base upon which to stand, we will be on the right track of equality. So if we want to know whether the principles we are using in our revolution are desirable or not and whether they are following the right line, we must first study carefully the history of European revolutions from their very beginnings. And if people want to understand thoroughly our Three Principles and to know whether they are really a good thing, suitable to the needs of our country, if they want to be able to believe in our Three Principles and never waver in their faith, they, too, must study carefully the history of Western revolutions from their inception.

Without democracy, liberty and equality would have been but empty terms. The origin of democracy lies far back in history; two thousand or more years ago Rome

之後，常常被平等自由引入歧路。我們的三民主義能够實行，真有自由平等。要甚麼方法才能够歸正軌呢？像第二圖，把平等線放在平頭上，是不合乎平等正軌的，要像第三圖，把平等線放在立足點，才算合乎平等的正軌。所以我們革命，要知道所用的主義，是不是適當，是不是合乎正軌，非先把歐美革命的歷史，源源本本來研究清楚不成功。人民要澈底明白我們的三民主義，是不是的的確確有好處，是不是合乎國情，要能够信仰我們的三民主義，始終不變，也非把歐美革命的歷史，源源本本來研究清楚不成功。

如果沒有民權，平等自由不過是一種空名詞。講到民權的來歷，發源是很遠的，不是近來才發生的，兩千多年

and Greece already had ideas of people's rights and were democratic states. South of the Mediterranean, at the same time was another republic called Carthage, and several small states which sprang up in succession afterwards were also republics. Although Rome and Greece of that day were democracies in name, in reality they had not attained to true liberty and equality. The people's sovereignty had not been applied. Greece had the slave system: the nobility all owned many slaves; in fact, two thirds of all the population were slaves. The warriors of Sparta were each given five slave attendants by the state. So in Greece the people with sovereign rights were a small minority: the large majority had no rights. The same thing was true in Rome. So Greece and Rome two thousand years ago were republics only in name; still having their slave system, they could not realize the ideal of liberty and equality. Not until the United States, sixty years ago, freed her slaves, smashed the slave system, and made the equality of mankind a reality did the hope of true liberty and equality begin to appear in modern democracy. True liberty and equality stand upon democracy and are dependent upon democracy.

以前，希臘羅馬便老早有了這種思想。當時希臘羅馬，都是共和國家，同時地中海的南方，有一個大國叫做克塞支，也是一個共和國，後來有許多小國，繼續起來，都是共和國家。當時的希臘羅馬，名義上雖然是共和國家，但是事實上還沒有達到眞正的平等自由，因為那個時候，民權還沒有實行。譬如希臘國內便有奴隸制度，所有貴族都是畜很多的奴隸，全國人民差不多有三分之二是奴隸。斯巴達的一個武士，國家定例要給五個奴隸去服侍他，所以希臘有民權的人是少數，無民權的是大多數。羅馬也是一樣的情形。所以二千多年以前，希臘羅馬的國家名義，雖然是共和，但是由於奴隸制度，還不能夠達到平等自由的目的。到六十年前，美國解放黑奴，打破奴隸制度，實行人類的平等以後，在現在的共和國家以內，才漸漸有眞平等自由的希望。但是眞平等自由是在甚麼地方立足呢？要附屬到甚麼東西呢？是在

Only where democracy flourishes can liberty and equality permanently survive; there is no way to preserve them if the sovereignty of the people is lost. So the Revolutionary Party of China, in its inception, took liberty and equality as aims in its struggle but made Democracy —the Sovereignty of the People—its principle and watchword. Only if we achieve democracy can our people have the reality and enjoy the blessings of freedom and liberty. They are embraced in our principle of the People's Sovereignty, hence we are discussing them in connection with our main theme.

After struggling so hard and pouring out so much blood for liberty and equality, how highly should we expect Europe and America to value these principles! How careful they should be to weigh them and not recklessly to abuse them! But the truth is, as I have said before, that many evil practices have flowed from the newly acquired liberty of the West. It is more than one hundred years since the American and French revolutions secured equality. Has equality, too, been abused? I think it has. We cannot afford, after the experience of Western nations, to follow in

民權上立足的，要附屬於民權。民權發達了，平等自由，才可以長存，如果沒有民權，甚麼平等自由都保守不住。所以中國國民黨發起革命，目的雖然是要爭平等自由，但是所定的主義和口號，還是要用民權。因爲爭得了民權，人民方有平等自由的事實，便可以享平等自由的幸福。所以平等自由，實在是包括於民權之內，因爲平等自由是包括在民權之內，所以今天研究民權的問題，便附帶來研究平等自由的問題。

歐美革命，爲求平等自由的問題來戰爭，犧牲了無數的性命，流了很多的碧血，爭到平等自由之後，到了現在，把平等自由的名詞，應該要看得如何寶貴，把平等自由的事實，應該要如何審慎，不能夠隨便濫用。但是到現在，究竟是怎麼樣呢？就自由一方面的情形說，前次已經講過了，他們爭得自由之後，便生出自由的許多流弊，美國法國革命，至今有了一百多年，把平等爭得了，到底是不是和自由一樣，也生出許多流弊呢？依我看起來，也是一樣的生出許多流弊。由於他們已往所生流弊的

their tracks and fight only for equality. We must fight for democracy; if democracy prevails, we shall have true equality; if democracy languishes, we can never have equality.

In our revolution we must not talk only about getting equality; we must hold up the people's rights. Unless democracy is fully developed, the equality which we fight for will be only temporary and will soon disappear. But although our revolution does not make Equality its slogan, still we do include equality in the Sovereignty of the People. When equality is a good thing we will apply it; when it is an evil, we will do away with it. Only thus can we make democracy develop and use equality to advantage.

I once suggested that the people of the world might be divided, according to their natural endowments, into three groups: those who know and perceive beforehand, those who know and perceive afterward, and those who do not know and perceive—the discoverers, the promoters, and the practical men. If these three groups could use each other and heartily cooperate, human civilization would advance " a thousand miles a day."

Although Nature produces men

經驗，我們從新革命，便不可再蹈他們的覆轍，專為平等去奮鬭，要為民權去奮鬭。民權發達了，便有眞正的平等，如果民權不發達，我們便永遠不平等。

我們革命不能彀單說是爭平等，要主張爭民權。如果民權不能彀完全發達，就是爭到了平等，也不過是一時，不久便要消滅的。我們革命，主張民權，雖然不拿平等做標題，但是在民權之中便包括得有平等。如果平等有時是好，當然是採用，如果不好，一定要除去。像這樣做去，才可以發達民權，才是善用平等。

我從前發明過一個道理，就是世界人類其得之天賦者，約分三種，有先知先覺者，有後知後覺者，有不知不覺者。先知先覺者為發明家，後知後覺者為宣傳家，不知不覺者為實行家。此三種人互相為用，協力進行，則人類之文明進步，必能一日千里。

天之生人，雖有聰

with varying intelligence and ability, yet the human heart has continued to hope that all men might be equal. This is the highest of moral ideals and mankind should earnestly strive towards it. But how shall we begin? We will better understand by contrasting two philosophies of life— the selfish which benefits self and the altruistic which benefits others. Those who are out for themselves are continually injuring others with no pang of conscience. When this philosophy prevailed, intelligent and able men used all their powers to seize others' rights and privileges, gradually formed an autocratic caste, and created political inequalities—that was the world before the revolutions for democracy. Those who are concerned with benefiting others are glad to sacrifice themselves. Where this philosophy prevails, intelligent and able men are ever ready to use all their powers for the welfare of others, and religions of love and philanthropic enterprises grow up. But religious power alone is insufficient and philanthropy alone cannot remedy all evil. So we must seek a fundamental solution, effect a revolution, overthrow autocracy, life up democracy, and level inequalities. Hereafter we should harmonize the three types which I have described and give them all equal standing.

明才力之不平等，但人心則必欲使之平等，斯為道德上之最高目的，而人類當努力進行者。但是要達到這個最高之道德目的，到底要怎麼樣做法呢？我們可把人類兩種思想來比對，便可以明白了。一種就是利己，一種就是利人。重於利己者，每每出於害人，亦有所不惜。此種思想發達，則聰明才力之人，專用彼之才能去奪取人家之利益，漸而積成專制之階級，生出政治上之不平等，此民權革命以前之世界也。重於利人者，每每到犧牲自己，亦樂而為之。此種思想發達，則聰明才力之人，專用彼之才能，以謀他人的幸福，漸而積成博愛之宗教，慈善之事業。惟是宗教之力有所窮，慈善之事有不濟，則不得不為根本之解決，實行革命，推翻專制，主張民權，以平人事之不平了。從此以後，要調和三種之人，使之平等，則人人當以服務為目的，而不以奪取為目的。聰明才力愈大者，當盡其能力而服千萬人之務，造

Everyone should make service, not exploitation, his aim. Those with greater intelligence and ability should serve thousands and ten thousands to the limit of their power and make thousands and ten thousands happy. Those with less intelligence and ability should serve tens and hundreds to the limit of their power and make tens and hundreds happy. The saying, "The skillful the slaves of the stupid" is just this principle. Those who have neither intelligence nor ability should still, to the limit of their individual power, each serve one another and make one another happy. In this way, although men now may very in natural intelligence and ability, yet as moral ideals and the spirit of service prevail, they will certainly become more and more equal. This is the essence of equality.

千萬人之福。聰明才力略小者，當盡其能力以服十百人之務，造十百人之福。所謂巧者拙之奴，就是這個道理。至於全無聰明才力者，亦當盡一己之能力，以服一人之務，造一人之福。照這樣做去，雖天生人之聰明才力有不平等，而人之服務道德心發達，必可使之成為平等了，這就是平等之精義。

# LECTURE FOUR*

## 第 四 講

民 國 十 三 年 四 月 十 三 日 講

IN the preceding lectures we saw that Europeans and Americans have been engaged for two or three centuries in their struggle for democracy. To-day I want to speak about the measure of people's rights which they have won and the progress which they have made in democracy during this period. Look at the so-called pioneers of democratic government in the West, like the United States and France, whose revolutions took place over a century ago—how many political rights have the people really won? To the believer in democracy, it seems that the people have gained but very little power. Those who fought for the people's rights thought that they would reach the democratic ideal at once, so they sacrificed everything and pooled all their rescurces of strength in a life and death struggle. But after they had conquered in battle, they found that they had gained much less power than they had hoped for during the revolution. They

* Delivered on April 13, 1924.

我們知道歐美人民爭民權，已經有了兩三百年，他們爭過了兩三百年，到底得到了多少民權呢？他們的民權，現在進步到甚麼地方。考察歐美的民權事實，他們所謂先進的國家，像美國、法國、革命過了一百多年，人民到底得了多少民權呢？照主張民權的人看他們所得的民權，還是很少。當時歐美提倡民權的人，想馬上達到民權的充分目的，所以犧牲一切，大家同心協力，一致拚命去爭。到了勝利的時候，他們所爭到的民權，和革命時候所希望的民權，兩相比較起來，還是差得很多，還不能達到民權的充分目的。

58

had not yet attained to perfect democracy.

Take once more the American War of Independence against Great Britain. It took eight years for the colonies to win the war and to achieve their ideals of popular sovereignty. According to the Declaration of Independence, liberty and equality are natural and in-alienable rights. The American revolutionists had hoped to win complete freedom and equality, yet after their eight years of struggle they still did not enjoy many popular rights. Why? The great enemy to the people's sovereignty in the American colonies was the British king; his oppressions gave rise to a war of democracy against autocracy. Since the war resulted in victory for democracy, it seems that the people should have gained all their rights. But why was the democratic ideal not realized? Because, after independence had been won and autocracy had been overthrown, problems as to the administration of democratic government arose among its supporters. How far could popular sovereignty be actually applied? Here the fellow disciples of democracy began to differ in their opinions. As a result there was a division into two great parties. You have all heard of the illustrious leader of the

現在可以回顧美國對於英國的獨立戰爭，是一個甚麼情形。那個戰爭，打過了八年仗，才得到最後的勝利，才達到民權的目的。照美國獨立宣言來看，說平等和自由是天賦到人類的，無論甚麼人都不能奪去人人的平等自由。當時美國革命，本想要爭到很充分的自由平等，但是爭了八年，所得的民權還是很少。為甚麼爭了八年之久，只得到很少的民權呢？當初反對美國民權的是英國皇帝，美國人民受英國皇帝的壓迫，才主張獨立，和英國戰爭，所以那個戰爭，是君權和民權的戰爭。戰爭的結果，本是民權勝利，照道理講，應該得到充分的民權。為甚麼不能達到充分的目的呢？因為獨立戰爭勝利之後，雖然打破了君權，但是主張民權的人，便生出民權的實施問題，就是要把民權究竟應該行到甚麼程度？由於研究這種問題，主張民權的同志之見解，各有不同，因為

American Revolution, the father-statesman of the United States—Washington. But there were other heroes also who helped him in his struggle against Great Britain. Among these were Washington's secretary of the treasury, Hamilton, and his secretary of state, Jefferson. As these two men differed radically over methods of administration and as both had large followings, they became the founders of two absolutely different political parties. Jefferson's party believed that the people were endowed with natural rights and that if the people were given complete democratic power, they would be discriminating in the use of their freedom, would direct their power to the accomplishment of great tasks, and would make all the affairs of the nation progress to the fullest extent. Jefferson's theory assumed that human nature is naturally good, and that if the people under complete democratic rule sometimes do not express their natural virtue and do good but abuse their power and do evil, it is because they have met some obstacle and are for the time being forced to act that way. In short, every man is naturally endowed with freedom and equality and hence should have political power; every man is intelligent and if given political power to govern would do

見解不同，便生出內部兩大派別的分裂。大家都知道美國革命，有一個極著名的領袖叫做華盛頓，他是美國的開國元勳。當時幫助他去反抗英國君權的人，還有許多英雄豪傑，像華盛頓的財政部長叫做哈美爾頓，和國務部長叫做遮化臣，那兩位大人物，對於民權的實施問題，因為見解各有不同，彼此的黨羽又非常之多，便分成為絕對不相同的兩大派。遮氏一派，相信民權是天賦到人類的，如果人民有很充分的民權，由人民自由使用，人民必有分寸，使用民權的時候，一定可以做許多好事，令國家的事業充分進步。遮氏這種言論，是主張人性是善的一說。至於人民有了充分的民權，如果有時不能充分發達善性去做好事，反誤用民權去作惡，那是人民遇到了障礙，一時出於不得已的舉動。總而言之，人人既是有天賦的自由平等，人人便應該有政權，而且人人都是有聰明的，如果給他們以充分的政權，令個個都可

great things for the nation; if all the citizens would shoulder the responsibility for good government, the state would prosper long in peace. Such was the Jeffersonian party's faith in the rights of the people.

The policy proposed by Hamilton's party was directly opposed to Jefferson's ideas. Hamilton did not think that human nature was always perfect; and he felt that, if democratic power were given equally to all men, bad men would direct their political power to bad ends. And if corrupt individuals should get much of the power of the state into their hands, they would use the rights and privileges of the state for the selfish benefit and profit of their own party; they would not care a rap for any morality, law, justice, or order in the nation, and the final result would be either a "state with three rulers"—divided authority and want of unity—or mob rule, that is, liberty and equality pushed to excess and anarchy. Such an application of democracy would not advance the nation but would only throw it into disorder and make it lose ground. So Hamilton proposed that the political power of the state should not be given entirely to the people, but should be centralized in the government, in a central authority;

以管國事，一定可以做出許多大事業，大家負起責任來，把國家治好，國家便可以長治久安，那就是遮化臣一派對於民權的信仰。

至於哈美爾頓一派所主張的，恰恰和遮氏的主張相反。哈氏以爲人性不能完全都是善的，如果人人都有充分的民權，性惡的人便拿政權去作惡。那些惡人拿到了國家大權便把國家的利益自私自利，分到自己同黨無論國家的甚麼道德、法律、正義、秩序、都不去理會。弄到結果，不是一國三公，變成暴民政治，就是把平等自由走到極端，成爲無政府。像這樣實行民權，不但是不能令國家進步，反要搞亂國家，令國家退步。所以哈氏主張國家政權，不能完全給予人民，要給予政府。把國家的大權都集合於中央，普通人只能夠得到有限制的民權。如果給予普通人以無限制的民權，人人都拿去作惡，那種作惡的影響，對於國家，比較皇帝的作惡，還要利害

the common people should have
only a limited degree of democracy.
If the people should all have unlimited power and should use it for
evil, the effect upon the nation
would be far more serious than the
evil deeds of one king. A wicked
king still has many people to oversee him and restrain him, but a
people who get unlimited power
into their hands and use it for wicked purposes have none to oversee
and restrain them. Therefore
Hamilton declared that, as autocracy had to be restricted, so democracy must also be limited, and he
founded the Federalist Party which
advocated the centralization and
not the diffusion of sovereign power.

Before the War of Independence
the thirteen original colonies were
governed by Great Britain and were
unable to unite. Later, when they
found that they could not endure
the extreme despotism of the British
government, they resisted, and out
of their common aim a common
spirit was born. But after the war,
the colonies again divided and found
themselves unable to agree.

After the states had secured their
independence, they were no longer
troubled by enemies within, but
their three million people were
scattered throughout thirteen states
with not over two hundred thousand
in any one state, and the states did

62

得多。因爲皇帝作惡，
還有許多人民去監視防
止。一般人若得到了無
限制的民權，大家都去
作惡，便再沒有人可以
監視防止。故哈美爾頓
說：「從前的君權要限
制，現在的民權也應該
要限制」。由此創立一
派，叫做聯邦派，主張
中央集權，不主張地方
分權。

美國在獨立戰爭以
前，本有十三邦，都歸
英國統轄，自己不能統
一。後來因爲都受英國
專制太過，不能忍受，
去反抗英國，是大家有
同一的目標，所以當時
對英國作戰，便聯同一
氣。到戰勝了英國以後
，各邦還是很分裂，還
是不能統一。

美國獨立之後，國
內便沒有敵人。但是那
三百萬人，分成十三邦
，每邦不過二十多萬人
，各不相下，大家不能
統一，美國的國力還是
很弱，將來還是很容易

not get along well together. Since they would not unite, the nation's power was weak; it might easily be swallowed up by another European power. The future was full of dangers. Then the farseeing statesmen of the different states saw that they must increase their national strength tremendously if they wanted to avert the dangers ahead and establish a permanent naton. So they proposed that all the states unite and form one great state. Some advocated purely popular sovereignty and others purely national sovereignty as a means of bringing about union. The former group advocated local authority, the latter group advocated centralized authority and the limitation of the people's power. They wanted the states all to pool their own rights and powers in a strong central government, and so were called the Federalists. The fight waged between these two opposing groups by mouth and pen was long and bitter. Finally the Federalists who advocated the limitation of popular sovereignty won out, the states got together, formed a federal union, and promulgated the Constitution of the United States. From the beginning of the Republic until now the United States has used· this Constitution, which divides clearly the legislative, judicial, and executive

被歐洲吞滅，前途的生存是很危險的。於是各邦的先知先覺，想免去此種危險，要國家永遠圖生存，便不得不加大國力，要加大國力，所以主張各邦聯合起來，建設一個大國家。當時所提倡聯合的辦法，有主張專行民權的，有主張專行國權的。頭一派的主張，就是地方分權。後一派的主張，就是中央集權，限制民權，把各邦的大權力都聯合起來，集中於中央政府，又可以說是聯邦派。這兩派彼此用口頭文字爭論，爭了很久，並且很激烈。最後是主張限制民權的聯邦派佔勝利，於是各邦聯合起來，成立一個合衆國，公佈聯邦的憲法。美國自開國一直到現在，都是用這種憲法。這種憲法就是三權分立的憲法，把立法權司法權和行政權分得清清楚楚，彼此不相侵犯。這是世界上自有人類歷史以來，第一次所行的完全憲法。美國就是實行三權分立的成文憲法的第一個國家。世界上有成文憲法的國家，美國就是破天荒

powers of the government so that they do not encroach upon each other. It was the first complete constitution in human history and the United States was the first nation to adopt a written constitution separating the three branches of government. This constitution *is* what we call the Federal Constitution of the United States. Since the United States formed a federal union and adopted the Constitution, it has become the wealthiest and, since the European War, the most powerful nation in the world.

Because the United States started on the road to its present position of wealth and power from a federal constitution which yet leaves the local affairs of the people to state control, a group of Chinese intellectuals and scholars during the last decade have been proposing that China, in order to be wealthy and strong, must also form a federal union. They have thought to solve China's present problems, but they have not made a fundamental comparison of the conditions in the United States and in China; their only argument is that since a federal union made the United States wealthy and strong, and since China's great hope is to be wealthy and strong, therefore we should have a federal union of the pro-

64

的頭一個：這個憲法，我們叫做美國聯邦憲法。美國自結合聯邦成立憲法以後，便成世界上頂富的國家，經過歐戰以後，更成世界上頂強的國家。

因為美國達到了今日這樣富強，是由於成立聯邦憲法。地方人民的事，讓各邦分開自治。十多年來，我國一般文人志士，想解決中國現在的問題，不根本上拿中美兩國的國情來比較，只就美國富強的結果而論，以為中國所希望的，不過是在國家富強，美國之所以富強，是由於聯邦，中國要像美國一樣的富強，便應該聯省，美國聯邦制度的根本好處，是由於各邦自定憲法，分邦自治。我們要學美國的聯邦制度，變為聯省，根本上便應該各省自定憲法，分省自治。等到省憲實行了以後，然後再行

vinces. The fundamental advantage of the American federal system came from the fact that each state already had a constitution and a government of its own. If we want to follow the United States' federal plan and form a union of provinces, all the provinces should first adopt constitutions and establish their own governments, then unite and decide upon a national constitution. In a word, we would have to take our already united China, divide it into twenty-odd independent units to correspond with the dozen or so independent American states over a century ago, and then weld them together again. Such views and ideas are utterly fallacious. We become mere parrots, repeating with our eyes shut what others tell us. Because the United States, with its federal system, has become the world's wealthiest and greatest power, we think that we must copy her system in order that China may be wealthy and strong. This is similar to what I have said before: while Westerners fought for democracy, they did not talk about democracy but about liberty and equality; so we Chinese in our revolution must take the Western slogans and cry that we are struggling for liberty and equality! All this is but blind following and foolish incomprehension. We see that the provinces in

聯合成立國憲。質而言之，就是將本來統一的中國，變成二十幾個獨立的單位，像一百年以前的美國十幾個獨立的邦一樣，然後再來聯合起來，這種見解和思想，真是謬誤到極點，可謂人云亦云，習而不察。像這樣只看見美國行聯邦制度，便成世界頂富強的國家，我們現在要中國富強，也要去學美國的聯邦制度，就是像前次所講的歐美人民爭民權，不說要爭民權，只說要爭自由平等，我們中國人此時來革命也要學歐美人的口號，說去爭自由平等，都是一樣的盲從，都是一樣的莫名其妙。中國的各省，在歷史上向來都是統一的，不是分裂的，不是不能統屬的，而且統一之時就是治，不統一之時就是亂的。美國之所以富強，不是由於各邦之獨立自治，還是由於各邦聯合後的進化所成的一個統一國家。所以美國的富強，是各邦統一的結果，不是各邦分裂的結果。中國原來既是統一的，便不應該把各省再來分開。如

past history have been united, not separate, parts of China and have not been incapable of unified rule. Mcreover, the periods of unity have been the periods of good government; the periods of disunity, the periods of disorder. The United States' wealth and power have not come only from the independence and self-government of the original states, but rather from the progress in unified government which followed the federation of the states. Her wealth and power were the result of the union of the states, not of the division into states. Since China was originally unified we should not divide her again into separate provinces. If we say that the American federal system is the key to wealth and power, we are putting effect before cause.

When the thirteen American states secured their independence from England, they had absolutely no political unity, and the formation of a unified nation was a tremendously difficult task. So the debates between the parties of Hamilton and Jefferson were very fierce. When the Constitution was drawn up, each state was given freedom in casting votes. Finally, Hamilton's party won out and the Jeffersonian policy began to lose ground. Because the people of the country at the time when the Constitution

果以美國聯邦制度就是富强的原因，那便是倒果為因。

美國獨立時候的十三邦，毫不統一，要聯成一個統一國家，實在是非常的困難。所以哈氏和遮氏兩派的爭論，便非常之激烈，後來制成聯邦憲法，付之各邦自由投票，最後是哈氏一派佔勝利，遮氏一派的主張漸漸失敗。因為聯邦憲法成立之前，全國人有兩大派的主張，所以頒佈的憲法，弄成兩派中的一個調和東西。把全國的大政權，如

was framed were divided into these two great parties with different political theories, the Constitution which was finally promulgated was a document of compromise between the two parties. The important political powers which belonged to the central government were clearly defined in the Constitution, matters not regulated by the Constitution were left to local governments. The coinage of money, for example, was put under control of the central government, and local governments were not allowed to transgress upon this right. Foreign relations were delegated to the central government and no state could make a private treaty with a foreign country. Other matters, like national defense, the training of troops upon land and sea, the right to move and dispatch state militia, were all intrusted to the central government. Matters of detail which were not delegated by the Constitution to the central government were left to the individual states to regulate. This division of power was a compromise measure between the central government and the state governments. What rights did the people obtain out of this compromise?—Only a limited suffrage. The suffrage at that time was limited to the election of congressmen and of various state and local officials. The president

果是屬於中央政府的，便在憲法之內明白規定，若是在憲法所規定以外的，便屬於地方政府。比方幣制，應該中央政府辦理，地方政府不能過問。像外交，是規定由中央政府辦理，各邦不能私自和外國訂約。其餘像關於國防上海陸軍的訓練，與地方上民團的調遣等那些大權，都是歸中央政府辦理。至於極複雜的事業，在憲法未有劃歸中央政府的，便歸各邦政府，分別辦理。這種劃分，便是中央和地方的調和辦法。美國由於這種調和辦法，人民究竟得到了多少民權呢？當時所得的民權，只得到一種有限制的選舉權，在那個時候的選舉權，只是限於選舉議員和一部分的地方官吏，至於選舉總統和上議院的議員，還是用間接選舉的制度，由人民選出選舉人，再由選舉人才去選總統和那些議員。後來民權逐漸發達進步到了今日，總統和上議院的議員，以及地方上與人民有

and the senators were still elected indirectly by electors chosen by the people. Later the powers of the people were gradually enlarged until today the president, the senators, and all state and local officials who have any direct, important relation with the people are elected by direct popular vote. This is what we call universal suffrage.

Therefore, the evolution in the United States from limited to universal suffrage was very gradual. At first suffrage was enjoyed only by men. Only a decade or two ago women still did not have the right to vote. Twenty years ago the movement for woman suffrage became very strong in Europe and America. You all know that at that time many people felt that the women would not succeed in their struggle on the ground that they were inferior in intellect and ability to men and could not do all the things that men could do. So there were many opponents of woman suffrage not only among men but even among the women themselves. Even if all the women of the nation had fought violently for the right to vote, they could hardly have hoped to succeed. But seven or eight years ago the women of Great Britain, and not long afterward the women of the United States, were successful in their struggle. The

直接利害關係的各官吏，才由人民直接去選舉，這就叫做普通選舉。

所以美國的選舉權是由限制的選舉，漸漸變成普通選舉。但是這種普通選舉，只限於男人才能夠享受，至於女子在一二十年前，還是沒有這種普通選舉權。歐美近二十年以來，女子爭選舉權的風潮，非常激烈。大家都知道當時歐美的女子爭選舉權，許多人以為不能成功，所持的理由，就是女子的聰明才力不及男子，男子所能做的事，女子不能夠做，所以很多人反對。不但是男人很反對，許多女子自己也是很反對，就是全國的女人，都爭得很激烈，還料不到可以成功。到了七八年以前，英國女子才爭成功，後來美國也爭成功，這個成功的緣故，是由於當歐戰的時候，男子通同去當兵

cause was the European War. During the war, the men went into the army and spent their strength upon the battlefields. Consequently, much of the nation's business was left without men to care for it; there were not enough men to be officers and day laborers in the arsenals, to be engineers and conductors on the street cars, and to assume responsibility for the various kinds of business which required energetic attention at the home base. Women were called upon to fill men's jobs, and then those who had opposed woman suffrage, saying that women could not do the work of men, were stripped of their arguments and no longer dared to thwart the movement. The advocates of woman suffrage then won a complete victory and after the war the question was finally settled. From this we can see that the objective of the Western revolutions was originally democracy. The American War of Independence was a war for democrcay; after the war, however, comrades in the cause divided into two groups—one group advocating complete democracy, the other group advocating limited powers for the people but large powers for the state. Many later events went to prove that the common people did not possess the necessary intelligence and power to

，效力戰場，在國內的許多事業，沒有男人去做，像兵工廠內的職員散工，街上電車內的司機賣票，和後方一切勤務事宜，男子不敷分配，都是靠女子去補充，所以從前反對女子選舉權的人，說女子不能做男子事業，到了那個時候，便無法證明，便不敢反對，主張女子有選舉權的人，才完全佔勝利。所以歐戰之後，女子的選舉權，才是確定了。由此便知歐美革命的目標，本是想達到民權，像美國獨立戰爭，就是爭民權，戰爭成功之後，主張民權的同志又分出兩派，一派是主張應該實行充分的民權，一派是主張民權應該要限制，要國家應該有極大的政權，後來發生許多事實，證明普通人民的確是沒有知識沒有能力去行使充分的民權。譬如遮化臣爭民權，他的門徒也爭民權，弄到結果，所要爭的民權，還是失敗，便可以證明普通民眾不知道運用政權。由於這個原故，歐美革命，有了兩三百多年，向來的標題，都

wield complete sovereignty. That Jefferson and his disciples tried to obtain more rights for the people, but failed, shows that the common people did not know how to exercise political sovereignty. So, although the Western revolutions of these two or three hundred years have been carried out under the standard of democracy, the actual result has only been the attainment of suffrage for men and women.

The French Revolution also set up democracy as its goal. Scholarly advocates of democracy like Rousseau declared that all men had natural rights which kings and princes could not take away, and such theories gave birth to the revolution. When democracy began to be applied after the revolution, nobles and members of the royal house received so many injuries that they were unable to remain in France and had to flee to other countries. The French people were now making their first experiment in complete democracy; no one in the country dared to say that the people did not have intelligence and power; if one did, he would be accused of being a counter-revolutionist and would immediately be brought to the guillotine. The result was that a mob tyranny was instituted. Anarchy followed, society was panic-stricken, no one

是爭民權，所爭得的結果，只得到男女選舉權。

講到歐洲的法國革命，當時也是主張爭民權。所以主張民權的學者，像盧梭那些人，便說人人有天賦的權利，君主不能侵奪。用於盧梭的學說，便發生法國革命。法國革命以後，就實行民權。於是一般貴族皇室，都受大害，在法國不能立足，便逃亡到外國。因爲法國人民，當時拿充分的民權去做頭一次的試驗，全國人都不敢說民衆沒有知識，沒有能力，如果有人敢說那些話，大家便說他是反革命，馬上就要上斷頭臺。所以那個時候，便成暴民專制，弄到無政府，社會上極爲恐慌，人人朝不保夕。就是眞革命黨，也有時因爲一言不愼，和

was sure of his life from morning till evening. Even a regular member of the revolutionary party might, because of a careless word which offended the multitude, be sentenced to death. In this experiment at pure democracy, not only were many princes, lords, and nobles killed, but not a few ardent revolutionists of the time, like Danton, were put to death by the populace because of some word that did not please them. When the French people afterwards came to realize that such a state of affairs was too oppressive, many who had been eager supporters of democracy grew despondent and cold, turned against democratic government, and supported Napoleon for emperor. Democracy now met a great obstacle. Not from autocracy: the democratic movement had already become powerful and, as I have been saying, the world had reached the age of democracy. It stood to reason that democracy would steadily advance. Why, then, after democracy had overthrown autocracy, did such barriers to the progress of democracy arise? What created them? One cause was the attitude of the conservative supporters of democracy who advocated definite limitation of the people's sovereignty and the centralization of the state's power, rather than

大衆的意見不對，便要受死刑。故當法國試驗充分民權的時期，不但是王公貴族，被人殺了的是很多，就是平時很熱心的革命志士，像丹頓一流人物一樣，因爲一言不合，被人民殺了的也是很不少。後來法國人民看到這樣的行爲，是過於暴虐，於是從前贊成民權的人，反變成心灰意冷，來反對民權，擁護拿破崙做皇帝，因此生出民權極大的障礙。這種障礙，不是由民權發生的。在一百年以前，民權的風潮，便已經是很大，像前幾次所講的情形，現在世界潮流已達到了民權的時代，照道理推測，以後應該一天發達一天，爲甚麼到民權把君權消滅了以後，反生出極大的障礙呢？是甚麼原因造成的呢？一種原因，是由於贊成民權所謂穩健派的人，主張民權要有一定的限制。這派是主張國家集權。不主張充分民權，這派對於民權的阻力，還不甚大。阻礙民權的進步，也不很多。最爲民權障礙的人，還是主張充分民權

complete democracy. But this group was not powerful and did not impede the progress of democracy very seriously. The real obstructionists were the believers in absolute democracy. When, during the French Revolution, the people secured complete power, they no longer wanted leaders and they put to death many of the wise and able ones. The groups of violent followers who were left were devoid of clear perception and were easily made tools of by others. Without their "good ears and eyes" the people of the nation were unable to distinguish who was right and who was wrong in any issue that arose; only let someone incite them and everyone would blindly follow. Such a state of affairs was extremely perilous. So when the people awoke to it in the course of time, they did not dare to advocate democracy again. Out of this reaction against democracy developed a great obstacle to the progress of democracy, an obstacle created by the very people who advocated people's rights.

Since the American and the French Revolution, democratic ideals have been spreading steadily throughout the world. The newest theories of democracy owe their real origin, however, to Germany. The German mind has always been rich

的人，像法國革命時候，人民拿到了充分的民權，便不要領袖，把許多有知識有本事的領袖，都殺死了，只剩得一般暴徒，那般暴徒，對於事物的觀察既不明瞭，又很容易被人利用，全國人民既是沒有好耳目，所以發生一件事，人民都不知道誰是誰非，只要有人鼓動，便一致去盲從附和，像這樣的現象，是很危險的。所以後來人民都覺悟起來，便不敢再主張民權。由於這種反動力，便生出了民權的極大障礙，這種障礙，是由於主張民權的人自招出來的。

世界上經過了美國，法國革命之後，民權思想便一日發達一日。但是根本講起來，最新的民權思想，還是發源於德國。德國的人心，向來富於民權思想，所

in democratic ideas; labor unions are numerous in Germany. Democratic philosophy developed early in Germany, but up to the time of the European War it had not produced as much fruit as in France or Great Britain. The reason was that the methods used by the German government in dealing with democracy were different from those used by the British government; therefore, the results attained were also different. What were the methods used by the German government? Who hindered the growth of democracy in Germany? Many students say that the setback began with Bismarck.

From the establishment of the German Confederation until before the European War, Germany was the strongest state in the world. She was the master of Europe and the nations of Europe followed her as a leading horse. Germany was raised to her eminent position entirely by the creative arm of Bismarck. Within twenty years after he had taken charge of the government, Bismarck transformed a weak Germany into a powerful state. After such an achievement, democracy while it flourished in Germany did not have sufficient strength to challenge the government.

While Bismarck was in power, he not only dominated the world in

以國內的工黨，便非常之多。德國的民權思想，發達本早，但到歐戰以前，民權的結果，還不及法國、英國。這個理由，是因為德國對付民權所用的手段，和英國不同，所以得來的結果，也是不同，從前德國對付民權是用甚麼手段呢？德國是誰阻止民權的發達呢？許多學者研究，都說是由於俾士麥。

德國自聯邦成立了之後，到歐戰以前，是世界上最強的國家，執歐洲的牛耳。歐洲各國的事，都惟德國馬首是瞻，德國之所以能夠達到那個地位，全由俾士麥一手締造而成。因為俾士麥執政不到二十年，把很弱的德國，變成很強的國家，有了那種大功業，故德國的民權，雖然是很發達，但是沒有力量去反抗政府。

在俾士麥執政的時代，他的能力，不但是

73

political and military affairs and in all kinds of diplomacy, but he also used consummate skill in dealing with the democratic movement and in winning victories over his own people. In the latter part of the nineteenth century, after the Franco-Prussian War, economic wars as well as wars for democracy began to break out. The hot passion for democracy was gradually cooling, but something else was being born —socialism. Socialism is similar to the Principle of the People's Livelihood, which I have been advocating. At that time German socialism had a very wide influence.

Socialism was originally closely related to democracy and the two should have developed simultaneously. But why did democratic ideas in Europe give rise to democratic revolutions, while the spread of socialist theories failed to give rise to economic revolutions?— Because the birth of socialism in Germany coincided with Bismarck's regime. Other men would certainly have used political force to crush socialism, but Bismarck chose to employ other methods. He knew that the German people were enlightened and that the labor organizations were firmly established; if he attempted the suppression of socialism by political force, he would only labor in vain. Bismarck

在政治，軍事和外交種種方面戰勝全世界，就是對於民權風潮，也有很大的手段，戰勝一般民眾，譬如到了十九世紀的後半，在德法戰爭以後，世界上不但是有民權的戰爭，並且發生經濟的戰爭。在那個時候，民權的狂熱漸漸減少，另外發生一種甚麼東西呢？就是社會主義。這種主義，就是我所主張的民生主義。德國的社會主義，在那個時候，便非常之發達。

社會主義本來是和民權主義相連帶的，這兩個主義發生了以後，本來應該要同時發達的。歐洲有了民權思想，便發生民權的革命。為甚麼有了那樣發達的社會主義，在那個時候，不發生經濟的革命呢？因為德國發生社會主義的時候，正是俾士麥當權的時候，在別人一定是用政治力去壓迫社會主義，但是俾士麥不用這種手段。他以為德國的民智很開通，工人的團體很鞏固，如果用政治力去壓迫，便是徒勞無功。當時俾士麥本是

74

had already been in favor of absolute control by a centralized authority. What methods did he use to deal with the socialists? The Socialist Party advocated social reforms and economic revolution. Bismarck knew that they could not be suppressed by political power, so he put into effect a kind of state socialism as an antidote against the Marxian socialists' program. At the time when Bismarck was seizing the reins of government in Germany, most of the railways in Great Britain and France were privately owned. Because the capital industries were owned by the wealthy, all the industries of the nation became monopolies of the wealthy class, and the many evils of an unequal distribution of wealth began to appear. Bismarck did not want such conditions in Germany, so he put into effect a state socialism; he brought all the railways of the country under state ownership and control and put all the essential industries under state management. He determined upon hours of labor and arranged for old-age pensions and accident insurance for the workers. These measures were items in the program of reform which the Socialist Party was trying to carry out; the farseeing Bismarck took the lead and used the state's power to accomplish them. More-

主張中央集權的獨裁政治，他是用甚麼方法去對付社會黨呢？社會黨提倡改良社會，實行經濟革命，俾士麥知道不是政治力可以打消的。他實行一種國家社會主義，來防範馬克思那般人所主張的社會主義。當俾士麥秉政的時候，英國、法國的鐵路，多半是人民私有，因為基本實業歸富人所有，所以全國實業都被富人龔斷，社會上便生出貧富不均的大毛病。俾士麥在德國便不許有這種毛病，便實行國家社會主義，把全國鐵路都收歸國有。把那些基本實業，由國家經營，對於工人方面，又定了作工的時間，工人的養老費和保險金都一一規定。這些事業，本來都是社會黨的主張，要拿出去實行的。但是俾士麥的眼光遠大，先用國家的力量去做了，更用國家經營鐵路、銀行和各種大實業，拿所得的利益去保護工人，令全國工人都是心滿意足，德國從前每年都有幾十萬工人到外國去做工，到了俾

over, he used the profits from the state-managed railways, banks, and other businesses for the protection of workers, which of course made the workers very contented. Before this, several hundred thousand workers had been leaving Germany for other countries every year, but after Bismarck's economic policy was put into effect, not only did no more German workers leave but many came from other countries to work in Germany. Bismarck met socialism by anticipating it and by taking precautions against it, rather than by a head-on attack upon it; by invisible means he caused the very issues for which the people were struggling to dissolve. When there was nothing left for the people to fight for, revolutions naturally did not break out. This was the artful method by which Bismarck resisted democracy.

Looking now at the whole history of democratic progress, we see that the first setback occurred after the American Revolution when the supporters of democracy split into two camps, Jefferson's group advocating absolute democracy and Hamilton's group centralization of power in the government, and when the policy of centralization won out. The second setback occurred during the French Revolution when the people secured complete sovereignty but

士麥經濟政策成功時候，不但沒有工人出外國去做工，並且有許多外國工人進德國去做工。傳士麥用這樣方法，對待社會主義，是用先事防止的方法，不是用當衝打消的方法。用這種防止的方法，就是在無形中消滅人民要爭的問題，到了人民無問題可爭，社會自然不發生革命，所以這是傳士麥反對民權的很大手段。

現在就世界上民權發達一切經過歷史講：第一次是美國革命，主張民權的人分成哈美爾頓和遮化臣兩派，遮化臣主張極端的民權，哈美爾頓主張政府集權，後來主張政府集權派佔勝利，是民權的第一次障礙。第二次是法國革命，人民得到了充分的民權，拿去濫用，變成了暴民政治，是民權的

abused it and changed it into mob rule. The third setback occurred when Bismarck checked the people's power with his clever scheming. Democratic thought in the West has passed through these phases and has met these setbacks, yet, contrary to all expectation, it has of its own accord still moved forward and no human power has been able to thwart it or to hasten it. To-day democracy has become the great world problem, and the scholars of the world, whether conservative or progressive, all realize that the democratic idea cannot be suppressed. But as democracy develops, it will be inevitably abused in the same way as liberty and equality have been abused.

To sum up: the European and American struggles for liberty and equality bore fruit in democracy: after democracy prevailed, it was much abused. Before the development of democracy, the Western nations tried to suppress it and to destroy it with autocratic power. When autocracy had been overthrown, the followers of democracy became the obstructionists of democracy. When democracy was realized, it produced many evils, and a greater obstacle thus resulted. Finally Bismarck saw that the people could not be downed in their

第二次障礙。第三次是俾士麥用最巧的手段，去防止民權，成了民權的第三次障礙。這就是民權思想在歐美發達以來所經過的一切情形。但是民權思想，雖然經過了三個障礙，還是不期而然，自然去發達，非人力所能阻止，也非人力所能助長，民權到了今日，成世界上的大問題。世界上的學者無論是守舊派或者是革新派，都知道民權思想是不能消滅的，不過在發達的時候，民權的流弊還是免不了的，像從前講平等自由也生出流弊一樣。

總而言之，歐美從前爭平等自由，所得的結果是民權，民權發達了之後，便生出許多流弊。在民權沒有發達之先，歐美各國都想壓止他，要用君權去打消民權。君權推倒了之後，主張民權的人便生出民權的障礙，後來實行民權，又生出許多流弊，更為民權的障礙。最後俾士麥見到人民主張民權，知道不能壓止，便用國家的力量去替代人

77

desire for democracy, so he employed the power of the state as a substitute for the people's power and put into effect a state socialism; this policy also obstructed the march of democracy.

Tracing the beginnings of applied democracy, we see the American people after their revolution winning first the right to vote. At that time Westerners thought that democracy meant suffrage and that was all. If all the people without regard to social status, wealth, or intellectual capacity had the right to vote, democracy had reached its final goal. But what has been happening in the three or four years since the European War? In spite of many set backs, democracy is still moving forward and cannot be checked. Recently the people of Switzerland have won, in addition to the rights to vote, the rights of initiative and referendum. If the people have the right to choose their officials, they should also have the right to initiate and amend the laws. The rights of initiative and referendum are related to the enactment of laws. If a majority of the people think that a certain law will be beneficial, they can then propose it—this is the right of initiative; if they feel that a certain law is disadvantageous to

民，實行國家社會主義，這也是民權的障礙。

推到實行民權的原始，自美國革命之後，人民所得的頭一個民權，是選舉權，當時歐美人民以為民權就是選舉權算了，如果人民不論貴賤，不論貧富，不論賢愚，都得到了選舉權，那就算民權是充分的達到了目的。至於歐戰後三四年以來，又究竟是怎麼樣呢？當中雖然經過了不少的障礙，但是民權仍然是很發達，不能阻止。近來瑞士的人民，除了選舉權以外，還有創制權和複決權。人民對於官吏有權可以選舉，對於法律也應該有權可以創造修改。創制權和複決權便是對於法律而言的。大多數人民對於一種法律，以為很方便的，便可以創制，這便是創制權。以為很不方便的，便可以修改。修改便是複決權。故瑞士人民比較別國人民多得了兩種民權，一共有三種民權，不只

them they can amend it—this is the right of referendum. The Swiss people have thus two more popular rights than other peoples, altogether three. Some of the newly developed states in the northwestern part of the United States have, in recent years, gained another right besides those of the Swiss people—the right of recall of officials. Although the enjoyment of this right is not universal throughout the United States, yet several states have practiced it, so many Americans enjoy the four popular rights—suffrage, recall, initiative, and referendum. In some of the northwestern states they have been applied with great success, and some day they may be applied throughout the United States and perhaps throughout the world. In the future, any nation which wants complete democracy must certainly follow the example of these American states which have given four rights to the people. Do these four rights, when applied, fully solve the problems of democracy? World scholars, seeing that, although people have these four ideals of popular rights, yet the problem of democracy is not fully solved, say that it is only a matter of time. Ideas of direct popular rule, they consider, have developed but recently. The old theocracy lasted

一種民權。近來美國西北幾邦新開闢地方的人民，比較瑞士人民更多得一種民權，那種民權是罷官權。在美洲各邦之中，這種民權，雖然不能普遍，但有許多邦已經實行過了。所以美國許多人民，現在得到了四種民權：一種是選舉權，二種是罷官權，三種是創制權，四種是複決權。這四種權在美國西北幾州，已經行得很有成績，將來或者可以推廣到全美國，或者全世界。將來世界各國有充分的民權，一定要學美國的那四種民權。由此四種民權，實行下去，將來能不能夠完全解決民權的問題呢？現在世界學者，看見人民有了這四種民權的思想，還不能把民權的問題完全來解決，都以為是時間的問題，以為這種直接的民權思想，發生尚不久。從前的神權經過了幾萬年，君權經過了幾千年。這些直接的民權，新近發生，不過是幾十年，所以在今日還是一個不能解決的大問題。

for tens of thousands of years; the old autocracy has lasted for thousands of years. This direct democracy is a very new thing; it has come only within the last few decades. No wonder it is still a great, unsettled issue!

What is the share of the people in the government in those nations which have the highest type of democracy? How much power do they possess? About the only achievement within the past century has been the right to elect and to be elected. After being elected as the representatives of the people, citizens can sit in Congress or Parliament to manage the affairs of state. All measures of national importance must be passed upon by Parliament before they can be put into effect; without Parliament's approval they cannot be carried out. This is called representative or parliamentary government. But does this form of government insure the perfect development of democracy? Before a representative system of government had been secured, the European and American peoples struggled for democracy, thinking that it would certainly be the highest type of popular sovereignty.

So the hope of foreigners that representative government will insure the stability and peace of

照現在世界上民權頂發達的國家講，人民在政治上是佔甚麼地位呢？得到了多少民權呢？就最近一百多年來所得的結果，不過是一種選舉和被選舉權。人民被選成議員之後，在議會中可以管國事，凡是國家的大事，都要由議會通過，才能執行，如果在議會沒有通過，便不能行。這種政體叫做「代議政體」，所謂「議會政治」。但是成立了這種「代議政體」以後，民權是否算得充分發達呢？在「代議政體」沒有成立之先，歐美人民爭民權，以爲得到了「代議政體」，便算是無上的民權。

外國人所希望的「代議政體」，以爲就是人類和國家的長治久安

the state is not to be trusted. Democracy as soon as it was born met with many difficulties; after it was applied it experienced many humiliations, but still it steadily grows. Yet the fruit of democracy has been only representative government; when this is achieved the nations think that the limit is reached.

But the democracy advocated in the Three Principles upon which the Kuomintang proposes to reconstruct China is different from Western democracy. When we use Western history as material for study, we are not copying the West entirely or following in its path. We will use our Principle of the People's Sovereignty and remake China into a nation under complete popular rule, ahead of Europe and America.

之計。那是不足信的。民權初生，本經過了許多困難，後來實行，又經過了許多挫折，還是一天一天的發達，但是得到的結果，不過是「代議政體」。各國到了「代議政體」，就算是止境。

但是我們國民黨提倡三民主義來改造中國，所主張的民權，是和歐美的民權不同，我們拿歐美已往的歷史來做材料，不是要學歐美，步他們的後塵，是用我們的民權主義，把中國改造成一個「全民政治」的民國，要駕乎歐美之上。

## LECTURE FIVE*

### 第 五 講

民國十三年四月二十日講

THE Chinese people's ideas of political democracy have all come from the West, so in carrying forward our Revolution and in reforming our government we are imitating Western methods. Why? Because we see that Western civilization has been progressing by leaps and bounds, and that it is in every way more advanced than Chinese civilization.

Take other machinery which serves the needs of daily life and methods which are used in agriculture, industry, and business—the West has advanced far beyond China.

So, ever since the Roxer defeat,** Chinese thinkers have felt that, to make China strong and able to avenge the shame of the Peking Protocol, they must imitate foreign countries in everything. Not only must they learn material science from the West, but also political and social science. Thus, since the Boxer uprising the Chinese have lost all con-

中國人的民權思想，都是由歐美傳進來的，所以我們近來實行革命，改革政治，都是做效歐美。我們為甚麼要做效歐美呢？因為看見了歐美近一百年來的文化，雄飛突進，一日千里，種種文明都是比中國進步得多。

關於人類日常生活的機器，和農工商所用的種種方法，也沒有不是比中國進步得多的。

所以從義和團失敗以後，中國一般有思想的人，便知道要中國強盛，要中國能夠昭雪北京城下之盟的那種大恥辱，事事便非做效外國不可。不但是物質科學要學外國，就是一切政治社會上的事都要學外國，所以經過義和團之

* Delivered on April 20, 1924.
** 1900

fidence in their own power, and a higher and higher respect has been paid to foreign countries. As a result of this imitation of and respect for foreign nations, China has taken in a lot of foreign ideas. Hence Chinese wanted nothing from old China; everything must be modeled after the West. If we heard of anything foreign, we ran to copy it and tried to use it in China. Democracy also met with this abuse. After the Revolution of 1911, the whole country went mad and insisted upon applying in China the political democracy which Westerners talked about, without any study of its real meaning. In the last few lectures I described in detail the history of the democratic struggle in the West and the results which followed the victory of democracy. From these studies we saw that democratic rule had not been fully carried out in the West and that democracy had met with many obstacles in its onward march. Now China is proposing to practice democracy. If we imitate the West, we will have to imitate Western methods. But there is no fundamental solution as yet in Western politics of the problem of democracy; it is still a serious issue. Westerners who are using the newest scholarship to aid them in finding a solution have not made any

後，中國人的自信力便完全失去，崇拜外國的心理，便一天高過一天。由於要崇拜外國，倣效外國，便得到了很多的外國思想。因為信仰外國，所以把中國的舊東西都不要，事事都是倣效外國，只要聽到說外國有的東西，我們便要去學，便要拿來實行。對於民權思想，也有這種流弊，革命以後，舉國如狂，總是要拿外國人所講的民權，到中國來實行。至於民權究竟是甚麼東西，也不去根本研究。前幾次所講的情形，是把外國爭民權的歷史和勝利之後，所得的甚麼結果，詳細的說明。由於那幾次的研究，便知民權政治，在外國也不能夠充分實行，進行民權，在中途也遇到了許多障礙。現在中國主張實行民權，要倣效外國，便要倣效外國的辦法，但是民權問題在外國政治上，至今沒有根本辦法，至今還是一個大問題。就是外國人拿最新發明的學問，來研究民權，解決民權問題，在學理一方面，根本上也沒有好發

worth-while discoveries in democratic theory, nor have they found any satisfactory answer to the difficulties of democracy. So the methods of Western democracy cannot be our model or guide.

In the last two or three centuries, Europe and America have passed through many revolutions and their political progress has been much more rapid than China's, yet the Western political treatises do not show much advance upon the past. For instance, there lived in Greece two thousand years ago a great political philosopher named Plato; his *Republic* is still studied by scholars who say that it has much to contribute towards the political systems of to-day. It is not like battleships and drill manuals, which are discarded as worthless after ten years. From this we see that the physical sciences of the West undergo marked transformations from one decade to another; they are making rapid strides forward. But in the field of political theory, we find Plato's *Republic* written two millenniums ago still worthy of study and of great value in modern times. So the advance of Western political philosophy has not kept pace with the advance of Western material science. There has been no radical change in political thinking for two thousand years. If we copy West-

明，也沒有得到一個好解決的方法。所以外國的民權辦法，不能做我們的標準，不足為我們的師導。

　　歐美兩三百年來，經過許多次數的革命，政治上的進步雖然是比中國快得多，但是外國的政治書本，像二千多年以前，在希臘有一位大政治哲學家，叫柏拉圖，他所著的共和政體那本書，至今還有學者去研究，對於現在的政體，還以為有多少價值可以供參考，不像兵船操典，過了十年，便成無價值的廢物。由此便知外國的物質科學，每十年一變動，十年之前，和十年之後，大不相同，那種科學的進步是很快的。至於政治理論，在二千年以前，柏拉圖所寫的共和政體，至今還有價值去研究，還是很有用處。所以外國政治哲學的進步，不及物質進步這樣快的。他們現在的政治思想，和二千多年以前的思想，根本還沒有大變動。如果我們傲效外國的政治

ern government as we are copying Western material science, we shall be making a great mistake. The material civilization of the West is changing daily, and to keep up with it will be exceedingly difficult. But political thought in the West has advanced much more slowly than material civilization. The reason why Western democracy has not made more progress is that Western nations have not fundamentally solved the problem of administering democracy. We saw in the preceding lectures that the West has not yet found any proper method of carrying out democracy and that the truths of democracy have not yet been fully manifested. The democratic spirit has swollen like a noisy torrent within the last two or three centuries, in issues which men could not think through, the masses of the people have simply followed nature and have drifted with the tide. The recent growth of democracy is not an achievement of thoughtful scholarship but the result of a popular following of natural tendencies. For this reason, no fundamental method of directing democracy was worked out beforehand, the problem was not considered from beginning to end, and so the Western peoples have met innumerable disappointments and difficulties half-

，以爲也是像倣效物質科學一樣，那便是大錯。外國的物質文明，一天和一天不同，我們要學他，便很不容易趕上。至於外國政治的進步，比較物質文明的進步，是差得很遠的，速度是很慢的。外國民權，所以沒有大進步的原因，是由於外國對於民權的根本辦法，沒有解決。由前幾次所講的情形，便知道歐美的民權政治，至今還是沒有辦法，民權的眞理，還是沒有發明。不過近兩三百年以來，民權思想逐漸膨脹，在人事上想不通的問題，大家便聽其自然，順着潮流去做罷了。所以近來民權的發達，不是學者從學理上發明出來的，是一般人民順其自然做出來的。因爲總是順其自然去做，預先沒有根本辦法，前後沒有想過，所以歐美實行民權，在中途便遭了許多挫折，遇了許多障礙。中國革命以後，要倣效歐美，實行民權。歐美的民權，現在發達到了代議政體，中國要跟上外國，實行民權，所以也有代議政體。

way on the road of democracy. Since the Revolution, China has wanted to follow the example of Europe and America and to apply political democracy. Since Western political democracy has developed to the point of representative government, China, too, must have a representative government! But the fine points of Western representative government China has not learned; the bad points she has copied tenfold, a hundredfold! China has not only failed to learn well from Western democratic government but has been corrupted by it.

From what I have already said, you must realize that Western democratic government does not have any fundamentally good method of application. So in our espousal of democracy, we should not entirely copy the West. Then what road shall we follow? For thousands of years Chinese social sentiments, customs, and habits have differed widely from those of Western society. Hence methods of social control in China are different from those used in the West, and we should not merely copy the West as we copy the use of their machinery. As soon as we learn Western machinery we can use it anytime, anywhere; electric lights, for example, can be installed and used in

但是歐美代議政體的好處，中國一點都沒有學到，所學的壞處，却是百十倍。所以中國學外國的民權政治，不但是學不好，反且學壞了。

大家知道歐美的民權政治，根本上還沒有辦法，所以我們提倡民權，便不可完全倣效歐美，我們不完全倣效歐美究竟要怎麼樣去做呢？中國幾千年以來，社會上的民情風土習慣，和歐美的大不相同。中國的社會既然是和歐美的不同，所以管理社會的政治，自然也是和歐美不同，不能完全倣效歐美，照樣去做，像倣效歐美的機器一樣。歐美的機器，我們只要是學到了，隨時隨地都可以使用，譬如電燈，無論在中國的甚麼房屋，

any kind of Chinese house. But Western social customs and sentiments are different from ours in innumerable points; if, without regard to cutoms and popular feelings in China, we try to apply Western methods of social control as we would Western machinery—in a hard and fast way—we shall be making a serious mistake. Hence this difference: in ways of controlling physical objects and forces we should learn from the West, but in ways of controlling men, we should not learn only from the West. The West long ago thought through the principles and worked out the methods of physical control, so we can wholly follow Western material civilization—we could even follow it blindly as we introduce it into China, and not go astray. But the West has not yet thought through its principles of government, and its methods of government have not been fundamentally worked out; so China to-day, when putting democracy into operation and reforming its government, cannot simply follow the West. We must think out a radically new method; if we only blindly follow others, we shall work serious injury to our national welfare and to the people's living. The West has its society; we have our society, and the sentiments and customs of the two are not the

都可以裝設，都可以使用。至於歐美的風土人情，和中國不同的地方，是很多的，如果不管中國自己的風土人情是怎麼樣，便像學外國的機器一樣，把外國管理社會的政治，硬搬進來，那便是大錯。是以管理物的方法，可以學歐美，管理人的方法，當然不能完全學歐美。因歐美關於管理物的一切道理，已經老早想通了，至於那些根本辦法，他們也老早解決了。所以歐美的物質文明，我們可以完全倣效，可以盲從，搬進中國來，也可以行得通。至於歐美的政治道理，至今還沒有想通，一切辦法在根本上還沒有解決，所以中國今日要實行民權，改革政治，便不能完全倣效歐美，便要重新想出一個方法。如果一味的盲從附和，對於國計民生，是很有大害的。因爲歐美有歐美的社會，我們有我們的社會，彼此的人情風土，各不相同，我們能夠照自己的社會情形，迎合世界潮流做去，社會才可以改良，國家才可以進步

same. Only as we adapt ourselves, according to our own social conditions, to modern world tendencies, can we hope to reform our society and to advance our nation. If we pay no attention to our own social conditions and try simply to follow world tendencies, our nation will decline and our people will be in peril. If we want China to progress and our race to be safe, we must put democracy into effect ourselves and do some radical thinking upon the best way to realize its ideals.

Can we find a real way to carry out democratic government? Although we cannot wholly copy Europe and America, yet we can observe them and study their experience in democracy very carefully.

Foreign scholars, in studying the historical facts of democracy, have deduced many new theories. One of the newest has been proposed by an American scholar, who says that the greatest fear of modern democratic states is an all-powerful government which the people have no way of checking, but yet the finest thing would be an all-powerful government in the employ of all the people and working for the welfare of all the people. This is

○如果不照自己的社會情形，迎合世界潮流去做，國家便要退化，民族便受危險。我們要中國進步，民族的前途沒有危險，自己來實行民權，自己在根本上，便不能不想出一種辦法。

我們對於民權政治，到底能不能夠想出辦法呢？我們要能夠想出辦法，雖然不能完全倣效歐美，但是要借鑑於歐美，要把歐美已往的民權經驗，研究到清清楚楚。

現在各國學者，研究已往民權的事實，得到了許多新學理，那是些什麼學理呢？最新的對於政治問題的，有一位美國學者說：「現在講民權的國家，最怕的是得到了一個萬能政府，人民沒有方法去節制他；最好的是得一個萬能政府，完全歸人民使用，為人民謀幸福」。

88

a very new theory: what is both feared and desired is an all-powerful government. First the theory declares that the people dread an all-powerful government which they cannot control, then it asks how an all-powerful government which will work for the welfare of the people can be secured, and how it can be made responsive to the will of the people. In many nations where democracy is developing, the governments are becoming powerless, while in the nations where democracy is weak, the governments are all strong. As I said before the strongest government in Europe within the past few decades was Bismarck's government in Germany. That was certainly an all-powerful government; it did not advocate democracy, for at first it opposed democracy, but yet it became all-powerful. Of the governments which have supported democracy not one could be called all-powerful. A certain Swiss scholar has said that since various nations have put democracy into practice, the power of government has declined, and the reason has been the fear on the part of the people that the government might secure a power which they could not control. Hence the people have always guarded their governments and have not allowed them power, lest they

這一說是最新發明的民權學理。但所怕所欲，都是在一個萬能政府。第一說是人民怕不能管理萬能的政府，第二說是爲人民謀幸福的萬能政府。要怎麼樣才能夠把政府變成萬能呢？變成了萬能政府，要怎麼樣才聽人民的話呢？在民權發達的國家，多數的政府都是弄到無能的，民權不發達的國家，政府多是有能的。近幾十年來，歐洲最有能的政府，就是德國俾士麥當權的政府，在那個時候的德國政府，的確是萬能政府。那個政府本是不主張民權的，本是要反對民權的，但是他的政府，還是成了萬能政府。其他各國主張民權的政府，沒有那一國可以叫做萬能政府。又有一位瑞士學者說：「各國自實行了民權以後，政府的能力便行退化。這個理由，就是人民恐怕政府有了能力，人民不能管理。所以人民總是防範政府，不許政府有能力，不許政府是萬能。所以實行民治的國家，對於這個問題，便應該想方法去解決。

become all-powerful. Therefore, democratic countries must find a solution for this difficulty, but the solution will not come until the people change their attitude towards government. The reason why the people have always been opposing government is because, after the revolutions, the liberty and equality thus obtained were overdeveloped, and certain groups abused them, setting no limits upon them and going into all sorts of excess, with the result that the government became impotent, and the state, although it had a government, became no different from a state without a government. The Swiss scholar whom I mentioned saw this evil train of events, and as a remedy proposed that the people should change their attitude towards government. What did he mean? What has the attitude of the people to do with government?

In China's long history, what has been the attitude of the people towards the government? As we study Chinese history, we find that the governments of Yao, Shun, Yu, T'ang, Wen Wang, and Wu Wang* are always lauded and held in admiration by the Chinese people; Chinese of every period hoped that they might have a government like

* Emperors of ancient China.

想解決這個問題,人民對於政府的態度,就應該要改變」。從前人民對於政府,總是有反抗態度的緣故,是由於經過了民權革命以後,人民所爭得的自由平等,過於發達,一般人把自由平等,用到太沒有限制,把自由平等的事,做到過於充分,政府毫不能夠做事。到了政府不能做事,國家雖然是有政府,便和無政府一樣。這位瑞士學者看出了這個流弊,要想挽救,便主張人民要改變對於政府的態度。他究竟要人民變成甚麼態度呢?人民的態度,對於政府有甚麼關係呢?

譬如就中國幾千年的歷史說,中國人在這幾千年中,對於政府是甚麼樣的態度呢?我們研究歷史,總是看見人稱讚堯、舜、禹、湯、文、武,堯、舜、禹、湯、文、武的政府,是中國人常常羨慕的政府,中國人無論那個時代

those, which would seek the welfare of the people. Before Western democratic ideas penetrated China, the deepest desire of the Chinese people was for emperors like Yao, Shun, Yu, T'ang, Wen Wang, and Wu Wang, that the people might enjoy peace and happiness. This was the old Chinese attitude towards government. But since our recent revolution, the people have absorbed democratic ideas and are no longer satisfied with those ancient emperors. They were all autocratic rulers, the people say, and do not deserve to be extolled even though they were splendid. This shows that the rise of democracy has developed an attitude of opposition to government among the people; no matter how good the government is, they are not content with it. If we let this attitude of mind continue without any attempt to change it, it will be exceedingly difficult for government to make any progress.

When we launched our revolution, we advocated the practice of democracy; and I have thought of a method to solve the problem. The method which I have thought of is a new discovery in political theory and is a fundamental solution of the whole problem. My proposition is similar to the thesis of the Swiss scholar that the attitude

，總是希望有那樣的政府，替人民來謀幸福。所以歐美的民權思想，沒有傳進中國以前，中國人最希望的就是堯、舜、禹、湯、文、武，以為有了堯、舜、禹、湯、文、武那些皇帝，人民便可以得安樂，便可以享幸福。這就是中國人向來對於政府的態度。近來經過了革命以後，人民得到了民權思想，對於堯、舜、禹、湯、文、武、那些皇帝，便不滿意，以為他們都是專制皇帝，雖美亦不足稱。由此便知民權發達了以後，人民便有反抗政府的態度，無論如何良善皆不滿意。如果持這種態度，長此以往，不想辦法來改變，政治上是很難望進步的。

我們革命，主張實行民權，對於這個問題我想到了一個解決的方法，我的解決方法，是世界上學理中第一次的發明，我想到的方法，就是解決這個問題的一個根本辦法。我的辦法，就是像瑞士學者近日的發明一樣，人民對於

of people to government must be changed, and the recent appearance of such theories in the West proves that the principle which I have advocated is right; namely, that a distinction should be made between sovereignty and ability* Western scholars have not yet discovered this principle. To make clear what I mean, I must first review my theory as to the classes of human society.

Upon what did I base my division of human society? —Upon the individual's natural intelligence and ability. I classified mankind into three groups. The first group are those who see and perceive first: they are the people of superior wisdom who take one look at a thing and see numerous principles involved, who hear one word and immediately perform great deeds, whose insight into the future and whose many achievements make the world advance and give mankind its civilization. These men of vision and foresight are the creators, the discovers of mankind. The second group includes those who see and perceive later :their intelligence and ability are below the standard of the first group; they cannot create

政府是改變態度，近日有這種學理之發明，更足以證明我向來的主張是不錯。這是甚麼辦法呢？就是權與能要分別的道理，這個權能分別的道理，從前歐美的學者都沒有發明過。究竟甚麼是叫做權與能的分別呢？要講清楚這個分別，便要把我從前對於人類分別的新發明再拿來說一說。

我對於人類的分別，是何所根據呢？就是根據於各人天賦的聰明才力。照我的分別，應該有三種人，第一種人叫做先知先覺，這種人有絕頂的聰明，凡見一件事，便能夠想出許多道理，聽一句話，便能夠做出許多事業，有了這種才力的人，才是先知先覺。由於這種先知先覺的人，預先想出了許多辦法，做了許多事業，世界才有進步，人類才有文明，所以先知先覺的人，是世界上的創造者，是人類中的發明家。第二種人叫做後知後覺，這種人的聰明才力，比較第一種人是次一等的，自己不能夠創造發明，只能夠跟隨摹做，第一種人已經做

---

* Ch'uan and Nen are difficult to translate by one phrase because of the various shades of meaning in different contexts. They convey the idea of "right" and "power" as well as "sovereignty" and "ability" and might be so rendered.

or discover but can only follow and imitate, learning from what the first group have already done. The third group are those who do not see or perceive: they have a still lower grade of intelligence and ability and do not understand even though one tries to teach them; they simply act. In the language of political movements, the first group are the discovers; the second group, the promoters; the third group, the operators. Progress in everything depends upon action, so the responsibility for the world's progress rests upon the third group.

For example, the construction of a large foreign-style building is not something which can be undertaken by the ordinary person. First there must be a construction engineer, who makes a complete estimate of the work and materials necesary for the desired building, and then draws a detailed plan for the contractor or foreman. The foreman first studies the plan carefully, then hires workmen to move materials and to work according to the plan. The workmen cannot read the plan; they merely work according to the foreman's directions and take his orders to put a brick here or to lay a tile there—simple tasks. The foreman, in turn, is unable to make complete estimates on the building or to draw a plan; he can only follow the plan

出來了的事，他便可以學到。第三種人叫做不知不覺，這種人的聰明才力是更次的，凡事雖有人指敎他，他也不能知，只能去行。照現在政治運動的言詞說，第一種人是發明家，第二種人是宣傳家，第三種人是實行家。天下事業的進步，都是靠實行，所以世界上進步的責任，都在第三種人的身上。

譬如建築一間大洋樓，不是一種尋常人能造成的，先要有一個工程師，把想做的洋樓，關於各種工程材料，都要通盤計算，等到通盤計算好了，便繪一個很詳細的圖，再把那個圖交給工頭去看，等到工頭把圖看淸楚了，才叫工人搬運材料，照那個圖樣去做，做洋樓的工人，都是不能够看圖樣的，只有照工頭的吩咐，聽工頭的指揮，或者是某處放一塊磚，某處加一片瓦，做那種最簡單的事。工頭又是不能够通盤計算去繪圖的，只有照工程師所繪的圖

made by the construction engineer and give orders to the workmen as to the laying of the brick and covering with tile. The construction engineer who designs the plan is the one who sees and perceives first; the foreman who reads the plan is the one who sees and perceives afterward, the workman who lays brick and tile is the one who does not see or perceive. The foreign buildings in every city depend upon these groups—engineers, foremen, and workmen—and upon their cooperative effort. All the great achievements of the world also depend upon these three groups, but the largest group is the one of practical operators who do not know or perceive. A smaller group are those who know and perceive afterward; the smallest group are those who know and perceive first. Without men who see and perceive ahead, the world would have no originators; without men who see and perceive later, the world would have no supporters; without men who do not see or perceive, the world would have no practical workers. The business of the world certainly requires first, initiators; next, many promoters; and lastly, a large number of operators, in order to be successfully accomplished. The progress of the world depends on these three types, and

94

，吩咐工人去砌磚蓋瓦。所以繪圖的工程師，是先知先覺，看圖的工頭，是後知後覺，砌磚蓋瓦的工人，是不知不覺。現在各城市的洋樓，都是靠工人工頭和工程師三種人共同做出來的。就是世界上的大事，也都是全靠那三種人來做成的。但是其中大部分的人，都是實行家，都是不知不覺，次少數的人便是後知後覺，最少數的人才是先知先覺。世界上如果沒有先知先覺，便沒有發起人。如果沒有後知後覺，便沒有贊成人。如果沒有不知不覺，便沒有實行的人。世界上的事業，都是先要發起人，然後又要許多贊成人，再然後又要許多實行者，才能夠做成功。所以世界上的進步，都是靠這三種人，無論是缺少了那一種人，都是不可能的。現在世界上的國家實行民權，改革政治，那些改革的責任，應該是人人都有份的。先知先覺的人要有一分，後知後覺的人要有一分，就是不知不覺的人也要有一分，我們要知道民

not one type must be lacking. The nations of the world, as they begin to apply democracy and to reform the government, should give a part to every man—to the man who sees first, to the man who sees later, to the man who does not see. We must realize that political democracy is not given to us by nature; it is created by human effort. We must create democracy and then give it to the people, not wait to give it until the people fight for it.

Since the West has not solved the difficulties of democracy, we cannot find a solution to-day by merely copying the West. We must look for a new way, and that new way depends, as the Swiss scholar said, upon a change of attitude towards government. But to secure this change of attitude we must distinguish clearly between sovereignty and ability. To help us in studying this distinction, let us review a few of the points mentioned in a former lecture. The first point is our definition of the people's sovereignty; briefly, it means the control of the government by the people. To explain this further: Who controlled the government in former times? Two ancient Chinese sayings, "One who does not hold a position under the government does not concern himself with the gov-

權不是天生的，是人造成的，我們應該造成民權，交到人民，不要等人民來爭，才交到他們。

歐美對於民權問題，還沒有解決的辦法，今日我們要解決民權問題，如果倣效歐美，一定是辦不通的。歐美既無從倣效，我們自己便應該想一種新方法，來解決這個問題。這個新方法，是像瑞士的學者最新的發明，人民對於政府要改變態度。但要改變態度，就是要把權與能來分開。權與能要怎麼樣分開呢？我們要把他研究到清楚，便應該把前幾次所講的情形，重提起來再說，第一件甚麼是叫做民權呢？簡單的說，民權便是人民去管理政治。詳細推究起來，從前的政治是誰人管理呢？中國有兩句古語說：「不在其位

ernment" and "The common people are not in the councils," show that political sovereignty used to be entirely in the hands of the emperor and had nothing to do with the people. To-day we who advocate democracy want to put the political sovereignty into the hands of the people. What, then, will the people become? Since China has had a revolution and has adopted a democratic form of government, the people should rule in all matters. The government now may be called popular government; in other words, under a republic we make the people king.

Looking back through the millenniums of Chinese history, the only emperors who shouldered the responsibility of government for the welfare and happiness of the people were Yao, Shun, Yu, Tʻang, Wen Wang, and Wu Wang; no others were able to use their office for the blessing of the the people. Of all China's emperors, only Yao, Shun, Yu, Tʻang, Wen Wang, and Wu Wang so fulfilled their duties of government that they could stand "unabashed before Heaven above and unashamed before men below." They were able to reach this high ideal and to elicit pæans of praise from succeeding generations because of two special qualities which they possessed—fine native ability,

，不謀其政」。又說：「庶人不議」。可見從前的政權，完全在皇帝掌握之中，不關人民的事。今日我們主張民權，是要把政權放在人民掌握之中。那麼人民成了一個甚麼東西呢？中國自革命以後，成立民權政體，凡事都是應該由人民作主的，所以現在的政治，又可以叫做民主政治。換句話說，在共和政體之下，就是用人民來做皇帝。

照中國幾千年的歷史看，實在負政治責任為人民謀幸福的皇帝，只有堯、舜、禹、湯、文、武，其餘的那些皇帝，都是不能負政治責任為人民謀幸福的，所以中國幾千年的皇帝，只有堯、舜、禹、湯、文、武能夠負政治責任，上無愧於天，下無怍於民。他們所以能夠達到這種目的，令我們在幾千年之後，都來歌功頌德的原因，是因為他們有兩種特別的長處：第一種長處，是他們的本領很好，能夠做成一個良政府，為人民謀幸福。第二種長處，是他

which enabled them to establish good government and to seek the welfare of the people; and noble character, "mercy to the people and kindness to all creatures, regard for the people as for the wounded and suffering, love for the people as for their own children." Because they possessed these two fine qualities, they were able to shoulder the full responsibility of the government and to reach their goal. These are the only emperors who have called forth reverence from posterity. Other emperors there have been— we do not know how many—and most of them, with their names, have been forgotten by posterity. Only Yao, Shun, Yu, T'ang, Wen Wang, and Wu Wang possessed great natural ability and noble character. Most of the others lacked ability and character, yet they wielded sovereign power.

You have all read a good deal of Chinese history; I am sure almost everyone here has read particularly *The Story of the Three Kingdoms.*\* We can find an illustration of our point in this book. Chukuh Liang, you remember, was a very scholarly and able statesman. The first chief that he served was Liu Pei; later he

們的道德很好，所謂「仁民愛物」，「視民如傷」，「愛民若子」，有這種仁慈的好道德。因為他們有這兩種長處，所以對於政治能夠完全負責，完全達到目的。中國幾千年來，只有這幾個皇帝，令後人崇拜，其餘皇帝不知道有多少，甚至於有許多皇帝，後人連姓名都不知道。歷代的皇帝，只有堯、舜、禹、湯、文、武，有很好的本領，很好的道德，其餘都是沒有本領沒有道德的多。那些皇帝，雖然沒有本領沒有道德，但是很有權力的。

大家都把中國歷史看得是很多的，尤其是三國演義，差不多人人都看過了，我們可以拿三國演義來證明。譬如諸葛亮是很有才學的，很有能幹的。他所輔的主，先是劉備，後是阿斗。阿斗是很庸愚的，

---

\* The period of Three Kingdoms, A.D. 122-265, was rich in military heroes and deeds of valor and has been immortalized by this well-known voluminous novel.

supported Ah Tou. Ah Tou was exceedingly stupid and did not have a bit of ability, which was the reason why Liu Pei just before his death said to Chukuh Liang, "If he is deserving of your support, support him; otherwise you may displace him." After Liu Pei's death, Chukuh Liang still showed his splendid character; although Ah Tou was worthless, Chukuh Liang aided him as loyally as ever, "wearing himself out with the duties of his office until he died." Thus, in the age of autocracy the ruler might have no ability but great power. Ah Tou and Chukuh Liang, in the period of the Three Kingdoms, make this very clear to us: Chukuh Liang had ability but not power; Ah Tou had power but not abliity. Ah Tou was incompetent, but he turned the affairs of state over to Chukuh Liang to administer. Chukuh Liang was exceedingly capable and so was able to build up a fine government in Western Shu (modern Szechwan); moreover, he was able to lead his troops six times across the Ch'i Mountains in a punitive expedition against the North and to establish a tripod of power along with the Wei and Wu kingdoms. The comparison between Chukuh Liang and Ah Tou helps us to understand the distinction between sovereignty and ability.

98

沒有一點能幹。因為這個原因，所以劉備臨死的時候，便向諸葛亮說：「可輔則輔之，不可輔則取而代之」。劉備死了以後，諸葛亮的道德還是很好，阿斗雖然沒有用，諸葛亮依然是忠心輔佐，所謂「鞠躬盡瘁，死而後已」。由這樣看來，在君權時代，君主雖然沒有能幹，但是很有權力，像三國的阿斗和諸葛亮，便可以明白。諸葛亮是有能沒有權的，阿斗是有權沒有能的，阿斗雖然沒有能，但是把甚麼政事都付託到諸葛亮去做，諸葛亮很有能，所以在西蜀能夠成立很好的政府，並且能夠六出祁山去北伐，和吳魏鼎足而三。用諸葛亮和阿斗兩個人比較，我們便知道權和能的分別。

In the age of autocracy fathers and elder brothers were kings, sons and younger brothers were heirs. Although they might have no ability at all, yet they could become kings some day. So incompetent men still had great sovereign power. Now that we have established a republic and acknowledge the people as ruler, will you look about to see to what groups our four hundred millions belong? Of course they cannot all be seers; most of them are not even follows of seers; the great majority are those who have no vision or foresight. Now democratic government depends upon the rulership of the people, hence our four hundred millions are very powerful. The people of the nation with sovereign power to control the government are these very four hundred millions. To whom can you compare all these political sovereigns? I think that they are very much like Ah Tou. In fact, each one of them is an Ah Tou with great sovereign power. Ah Tou had no ability, but Chukuh Liang did; so after Liu Pei's death, Western Shu was still well governed. Westerners now are opposing a beasts, which we formerly described, powerful government; the Swiss scholar, to remedy this defect, proposes that the people's attitude towards government should be

專制時代，父兄做皇帝，子弟承父兄之業，雖然沒有能幹，也可以做皇帝，所以沒有能的人也是很有權。現在成立共和政體，以民為主，大家試看這四萬萬人是那一類的人呢？這四萬萬人當然不能都是先知先覺的人，多數的人也不是後知後覺的人，大多數都是不知不覺的人。現在民權政治，是要靠人民作主的，所以這四萬萬人都是很有權的。全國很有權力能夠管理政治的人，就是這四萬萬人，大家想想現在的四萬萬人，就政權一方面說，是像甚麼人呢？照我看起來，這四萬萬人都是像阿斗。中國現在有四萬萬個阿斗，人人都是很有權的。阿斗本是無能的，但是諸葛亮有能，所以劉備死了以後，西蜀還能夠治理。現在歐美人民反對有能的政府，瑞士學者要挽救這種流弊，主張人民改變態度，不可反對有能的政府。但是改變了態度以後，究竟是用甚麼辦法呢？他們還沒有發明。我現在所發明的，是要權與能

changed—they should no longer be hostile to strong government. But what the next step is, after the popular attitude towards government is changed, they have not made clear. The principle which I am bringing out is that sovereignty must be distinguished from ability; without this clear distinction we cannot hope to change the people's attitude towards government. Ah Tou know that he was incompetent, so he turned over all the political authority of the kingdom to Chukuh Liang and ask Chukuh Liang to govern for him. So when Chukuh Liang handed in his memorandum upon the expedition to Ah Tou, he advised him to separate clearly the affairs of the palace and the affairs of the court. Ah Tou could execute the duties of the palace, but the duties of the court he could not perform alone, for they were duties of government. Chukuh Liang's distinction between palace and court was a distinction between sovereignty and ability. In governing the state, we must make the same distinction. How shall we do it? We shall succeed only as we take a long and dispassionate view of world affairs. Everybody now has a peculiar idea of government which has grown up out of millenniums of autocracy. In this long period of autocratic govern-

分開，人民對於政府的態度，才可以改變。如果權與能不分開，人民對於政府的態度，總是不能改變。當時阿斗知道自己無能，把國家全權託到諸葛亮，要諸葛亮替他去治理。所以諸葛亮上出師表，便獻議到阿斗，把宮中和府中的事要分開清楚，宮中的事，阿斗可以去做。府中的事，阿斗自己不能去做。府中的事，是甚麼事呢？就是政府的事，諸葛亮把宮中和府中的事分開，就是把權和能分開，所以我們治理國家，權和能一定要分開的。究竟要怎麼樣才可以分開呢？大家要拿一個遠大眼光和冷靜見解，來看世界上的事，才可以把他們分別清楚。大家此時對於政府，有一種特別觀念，這種觀念是怎麼樣發生的呢？是由於幾十年專制政體發生的。因爲幾千年的專制政體，多是無能力的人做皇帝。人民都是做皇帝的奴隸。在中國的四萬萬人，就做過了幾千年奴隸。現在雖然是推翻專制，成

ment, incompetent men have sat upon the throne while the four hundred millions have been their slaves; now, although autocracy is overthrown, a republic is established, and we are apparently free, yet the people have not gotten rid of their idea of autocracy and are still afraid that the government will oppress them as the emperors did. The fear of an imperial, despotic government makes them want to destroy the government and the attitude of hostility towards government develops. This present hostility is still the reaction from the old reverence for the emperor. In/ other words, from an attitude of extreme veneration for the emperor the people have swung to an attitude of opposition towards all government. The old worship of the emperor was wrong, of course, but the present hostility to all government is also wrong.

We must go back thousands of years in political history in order to understand how this wrong conception to-day can be broken down. Before the day of despotic emperors, China had the splendid rulers Yao and Shun, they both opened the throne to the people and did not attempt to keep it in their own family. Autocracy did not flower until after Yao and Shun; before

立共和政體，表面上固然是解放，但是人民的心目中，還有專制的觀念，還怕有皇帝一樣的政府來專制。因為再怕有皇帝一樣的政府來專制，想要打破他，所以生出反對政府的觀念，表示反抗政府的態度。所以現在人民反抗政府的態度，還是由於從前崇拜皇帝的心理反動生出來的，換句話說，人民對於政府的態度，就是由於從前崇拜皇帝的心理，一變而為排斥政府的心理。從前崇拜皇帝的心理，固然是不對，現在排斥政府的心理，也是不對的。

我們要打破這種不對的心理，便要回顧到幾萬年和幾千年以前的政治歷史，才可以看破。比方在專制皇帝沒有發達以前，中國堯舜是很好的皇帝，他們都是公天下，不是家天下，當時的君權還沒有十分發達，中國的君權，是從堯舜以後才發達的。

their time there was no autocracy to speak of, and men of ability who could work for the welfare of all and organize good government were appointed emperors. In the wild age of conflict between men and beasts, which we formerly described, there was no complete state organization; the people lived by clans and depended upon some skillful and strong man to provide for their protection. At that time people were afraid of the attack of venomous serpents and wild beasts, so they had to get an able man to assume the responsibility for protection. Responsibility for protection required ability to fight; the man who could overcome venomous serpents and savage beasts was considered the ablest, and, as men of that day had no weapons but bare hands and empty fists with which to fight, the one with the strongest body was raised by the people to the position of chief. China, however, had examples of others besides fighters who were made kings. Sui Jen Shih* bored wood for fire and taught the people to cook with fire; thus the dangers of eating raw vegetables and meat were avoided and many fine flavors to satisfy the palate were discovered. So the people made Sui Jen Shih king. Boring wood for fire and teaching

* Legendary figures in ancient Chinese history.

推到堯舜以前，更沒有君權之可言，都是奉有能的人做皇帝，能夠替大家謀幸福的人，才可以組織政府。譬如從前所講人同獸爭的野蠻時代，國家的組織沒有完全，人民都是聚族而居，靠一個有能的人來保護。在那個時候，人民都怕毒蛇猛獸來侵害，所以要奉一個有能的人，負保護的責任。當時保護的任務，就是在有能力去打，能夠打勝毒蛇猛獸的人，就是當時很有能幹的人，當時人同獸打，沒有武器，都是靠赤手空拳，要個人體魄很強壯，所以在當時體魄很強壯的人，大家便奉他做皇帝。除了會打的人可以做皇帝以外，中國還有例外，譬如燧人氏鑽木取火，教人火食，就可避去生食動植物的危險，復可製出種種美味，適於口腹之欲，所以世人便奉他做皇帝。鑽木取火，教人火食，是什麼人的事呢？就是廚子的事，所以燧人氏鑽木取火教人火食便做皇帝，就可以說廚子做皇帝。神農嘗

people to cook with fire were the work of a cook, so we may say that a cook became king. Shen Nung** tasted a hundred herbs and discovered many medicinal properties to heal diseases and to raise the dead to life—a wonderful and meritorious work—so they made him king. Tasting herbs is the work of a physician, and thus we may say that a physician became king. Hsien Yuan* taught the people to make clothes, so it was the tailor who became king; Yu Ch'ao Shih* taught the people how to build houses, and so the carpenter became king. So in Chinese history we find not only those who could fight becoming king; anyone with marked ability, who had made new discoveries or who had achieved great things for mankind, could become king and organize the government. Cooks, physicians, tailors, carpenters, and all others who had special ability had become king. The general psychology of the Chinese is that a man possessing marked ability should become king.

Since the time of Yao and Shun China's emperors have gradually become despots, wanting to monopolize the empire and refusing to let the people freely choose able men for the throne. If now our four hundred million people should be

百草，發明了許多藥性，可以治疾病，可以起死回生，便是一件很奇怪很有功勞的事，所以世人便奉他做皇帝。嘗百草是甚麼人的事呢？就是醫生的事，所以神農由於嘗百草便做皇帝，就可以說醫生做皇帝。更推到軒轅氏敎民做衣服也是做皇帝，那就是裁縫做皇帝，有巢氏敎民營宮室，也做皇帝，那就是木匠做皇帝。所以由中國幾千年以前的歷史看起來，都不是專以能夠打得的人才做皇帝，凡是有大能幹有新發明在人類立了功勞的人，都可以做皇帝，都可以組織政府。像廚子、醫生、裁縫、木匠那些有特別能幹的人，都是做過了皇帝的。中國人的一般心理，都以為是大本領的人，便可以做皇帝。

中國自堯舜以後，那些皇帝便漸漸變成專制，都要家天下，不許人民自由擁戴有本領的人去做皇帝，假若現在四萬萬人用投票的方法選舉皇帝，如果給以充

** Legendary figures in ancient Chinese history.

asked to elect an emperor by ballot, if they had complete power and freedom of choice without any outside interference, and if, at the same time, Yao and Shun should come to life again whom do you think they would elect? I think they would undoubtedly elect Yao or Shun. Chinese have not the painful and bitter feelings towards their emperors which Westerners have had, because despotism in China was never as severe as despotism in the West. In Europe two or three centuries ago the tyranny of kings had reached its limits: the people looked upon their rulers as they would upon an overwhelming deluge or a savage beast—with mortal terror. So the people wanted to reject not only their kings but everything closely connected with kings, such as government. Now that democracy prevails in the West and the people are in power, the rejection of government is truly easy. Would it not have been easy for Ah Tou of Western Shu to throw Chukuh Liang over-board? But if he had dismissed Chukuh Liang could the government of Western Shu have lasted very long, could the troops have been dispatched six times across the Ch'i Mountains to punish the North? Ah Tou realized all this, so he gave complete authority to Chukuh Liang; the setting

分的民權，人民能够自由投票，絲毫不受別種勢力的干涉，同時又有堯舜復生，究竟是選舉誰來做皇帝呢？我想一定是選舉堯舜來做皇帝。中國人對於皇帝的心理，不像歐美人對於皇帝的那樣深惡痛絕，因為中國皇帝的專制，沒有歐洲皇帝的那麼利害。歐洲在兩三百年以前，皇帝專制達到了極點，人民都視為洪水猛獸，非常的怕他，所以人民不但是對於皇帝要去排斥，就是和皇帝很相近的東西像政府一樣，也是一齊要排斥。歐美現在實行了民權，人民有了大權，要排斥政府，實在是很容易的。像西蜀的阿斗，要排斥諸葛亮，那還不容易嗎？如果阿斗要排斥諸葛亮，試問西蜀的政府能不能够長久呢？能不能够六出祁山去北伐呢？阿斗見到了這一層，所以便把政治的全權都付託到諸葛亮，無論是整頓內部是由他，南征是由他，就是六出祁山去北伐也是由他。我們現在行民權，四萬萬人都是皇帝，就是有四萬萬個

in order of the government, the suppression of the South the punitive expedition against the North, were all carried out by Chukuh Liang. We are now putting democracy into practice: the four hundred millions of China are the kings; they are the Ah Tous, and as Ah Tous they should naturally welcome Chukuh Liang to administer the government for them and to perform the great tasks of state. As Western nations have applied democracy, the people have developed an attitude of hostility towards government, and the fundamental reason is their failure to distinguish between sovereignty and ability. Unless we act upon this principle which I have set forth, we will simply follow in the ruts of the West. Only as the people, in accordance with the theory that I have set forth, see the clear difference between sovereignty and ability will hostility towards government cease and will government have a chance to develop. It should be very easy for China to make the distinction, for we can cite the precedent of Ah Tou and Chukuh Liang. If the government is a good one, we four hundred millions will let it be our Chukuh Liang and give all the authority of the state to it; if the government is bad, we four hundred millions can exercise the privileges

阿斗，這些阿斗當然是應該歡迎諸葛亮來管理政治，做國家的大事業。歐美現在實行民權，人民所持的態度，總是反抗政府，根本原因就是由於權和能沒有分開。中國要不蹈歐美的覆轍，應該要照我所發明的學理，要把權和能劃分清楚。人民分開了權與能，才不致反對政府，政府才可以望發展。中國要分開權與能，是很容易的事，因為中國有阿斗和諸葛亮的先例可援。如果政府是好的，我們四萬萬人便把他當作諸葛亮，把國家的全權都交到他們。如果政府是不好的，我們四萬萬人可以實行皇帝的職權，罷免他們，收回國家的大權。歐美人民對於政府，不知道分別權與能的界限，所以他們的民權問題，發生了兩三百年，至今還不能解決。

of kingship, dismiss it and take back the authority into our own hands. Westerners have not drawn a clear line between sovereignty and ability, so they have not yet solved the problems which have arisen out of democracy these two or three hundred years.

Let us make another comparison between the past and the present. In olden times those who could fight well were crowned king by all. To-day, when wealthy men organize a company or open a factory, they have to engage a man with natural capability to be general manager and to control the concern. This general manager is an expert who has the ability; the shareholders hold the authority or sovereignty. Within the factory, only the general manager gives orders; the shareholders simply keep a supervision over him. The people of a republic are shareholders, the president is general manager, and the people should look upon the government as an expert. With such an attitude, the shareholders can make use of the manager to improve the factory, turn out a large quantity of goods with a small capital, and make large profits for the company. But in none of the democratic states of the West do the people have such an attitude towards government, hence they cannot make use of gifted men

我們現在主張要分開權與能，再拿古時和現在的事實，比較的來說一說。在古時能打的人，大家便奉他做皇帝。現在有錢的那些人，組織公司，開辦工廠，一定要請一位有本領的人來做總辦，去管理工廠。此總辦是專門家，就是有能的人，股東就是有權的人，工廠內的事，只有總辦能夠講話，股東不過監督總辦而已，現在民國的人民，便是股東，民國的總統，便是總辦，我們人民對於政府的態度，應該要把他們當作專門家看，如果有了這種態度，股東便能夠利用總辦，整頓工廠，用很少的成本，出很多的貨物，可以令那個公司發大財。現在歐美民權發達的國家，人民對於政府都沒有這種態度。所以不能利用有本領的人去管理政府。因為這個原因，所以弄到在政府之中的人物都是無能，所以弄到民權政治的發達反是

to direct the government. As a result, the men in political life are generally incompetent, and democratic government is developing very haltingly. The reason lies in their failure to solve some of the basic problems of democracy. To solve them they must put the important affairs of the nation in the hands of capable men.

Westerners to-day are constantly making use of experts: in training soldiers they use experienced military men, in running their factories they use engineers, and in the administration of government they know that they ought to use specialists. They have not succeeded in doing so because they are not able to change the old, deep-rooted habits of the people. But in this new age a distinction must surely be made between sovereignty and ability. In many things we have to trust experts and we should not set limitations upon them. Take that very recent invention, now in such common use and so convenient—the automobile. When automobiles were first introduced twenty or thirty years ago, there were no expert chauffeurs to drive them or expert mechanics to repair them. I had a friend who bought an automobile and had to be both chauffeur and mechanic himself, which was a lot of trouble, as one could not be

很遲，民主國家的進步反是很慢，反不及專制國家的進步，推究此中原因，就是由於民權問題的根本辦法沒有解決，如果要解決這個問題，便要把國家的大事，付託到有本領的人。

現在歐美人無論做甚麼事，都要用專門家。譬如練兵打仗，便要用軍事家。開辦工廠，便要用工程師，對於政治也知道要用專門家。至於現在之所以不能實行用政治專家的原因，就是由於人民的舊習慣，還不能改變。但是到了現在的新時代，權與能是不能不分開的，許多事情一定是要靠專門家的，是不能限制專門家的。像最新發明在人生日用最便利的東西，是街上的汽車。在二十多年前，初有汽車的時候，沒有駕駛的車夫，沒有修理的工匠。我從前有一個朋友，買了一架汽車，自己一方面要做駕駛的汽車夫，又一方面要做修理的機器匠，那是很麻煩的，是很難得的方方面面都做好

expected to do all these things well. But now there are many chauffeurs and mechanics, and the owner of an automobile has only to pay out money and engage someone to drive or to repair his car for him. The chauffeurs and the mechanics are specialists in driving and in repair work, and they are essential if we use automobiles. The nation is a great automobile and the government officers are the great chauffeurs. When Westerners first won political sovereignty, they were like the wealthy owners of automobiles twenty years ago, who did not have suitable experts to help them and so had to do all the repairing and driving themselves. But now that there are so many gifted specialists, the sovereign people should engage their services; to drive and repair by themselves is only "seeking worry and trouble." In this illustration we can make a distinction, also, between the chauffeur who has skill but not sovereignty over the car, and the owner of the car who has sovereignty but not skill. The sovereign owner should depend upon the skillful expert to drive his car, and the same principle should apply in the vital affairs of the nation. The people are the owners; they must be sovereign. The government are specialists; they must be men of ability and skill.

108

的。到了現在，有許多的汽車夫和機器匠，有汽車的主人，只要出錢僱他們來，便可以替自己來駕駛，替自己來修理。這種汽車夫和機器匠，就是駕駛汽車和修理汽車的專門家，沒有他們，我們的汽車便不能行動，便不能修理。國家就是一輛大汽車，政府中的官吏就是一些大車夫，歐美人民始初得到了民權，沒有相當的專門家，就像二十多年以前有錢的人，得了一輛汽車一樣，所以事事便非靠自己去修理，自己去駕駛不可。到了現在，有了許多有本領的專門家，有權力的人民便應該要聘請他們，不然就要自己去駕駛，自己去修理，正所謂自尋煩惱，自找痛苦。就這個比喻，更可分別駕駛汽車的車夫是有能而無權的，汽車的主人是無能而有權的，這個有權的主人便應該靠有能的專門家，去代他駕駛汽車。民國的大事，也是一樣的道理，國民是主人，就是有權的人，政府是專門家，就是有能的人。由於這個理由

We are therefore to look upon all the officers of the government, from president and premier down to heads of departments, as specially trained chauffeurs; if they are able men and loyal to the nation, we should be willing to give the sovereignty of the state into their hands. We must not limit their movements but give them freedom of action; then the state can progress and progress with rapid strides. If, on the contrary, we attempt to take everything into our own hands, or to hamper our experts at every turn and not allow them freedom of action, the state can hardly hope to progress much and will move forward very slowly.

I can give you a very good illustration of this principle out of my own experience. Once, when I was living in Shanghai, I made an appointment for a conference with a friend in Hongkow. But when the day came, I forgot the appointment until just fifteen minutes before the set time. I was then living in the French concession, which is a long distance from Hongkow. It would be almost impossible to get there in fifteen minutes. In hot haste I called a chauffeur and asked him excitedly whether he could drive to Hongkow in fifteen minutes. He replied that he certainly could. So

，所以民國的政府官吏，不管他們是大總統是內閣總理是各部總長，我們都可以把他們當作汽車夫，只要他們是有本領，忠心為國家做事，我們就應該把國家的大權付託於他們，不限制他們的行動，事事由他們自由去做，然後國家才可以進步，進步才是很快。如果不然，事事都是要自己去做，或者是請了專門家，一舉一動，都要牽制他們，不許他們自由行動，國家還是難望進步，進步還是很慢。

要明白這個道理，我有一段很好的故事，可以引來證明。我從前住在上海的時候，有一天和一個朋友約定了時間，到虹口去商量一件事。到了那一天，把所約定的時間忽然忘記了，一直到所約定的時間十五分鐘之前，才記憶起來。當時我所住的地方是法國租界，由法國租界到虹口是很遠的，用十五分鐘的時間，很不容易趕到，我便着急起來，找着汽車夫，慌忙的問他說：「在十五

I took my seat in the automobile and we started for the appointed place. I was very familiar with the streets of Shanghai; the trip from the French concession to Hongkow is somewhat like that from Shakee to Tungshan (in Canton) which you can cut short by going through the Bund and Ch'uan Lung K'ou. But my chauffeur did not go, let us say, by the Bund and Ch'uan Lung K'ou; he first went down Fungning Road, turned through Taoteksun Road, and drove through the small North Gate before he reached the Great East Gate and then Tungshan. The automobile was flying along and making such a noise that I could not speak to the chauffeur; I was much puzzled, however, and angry at the chauffeur, because I thought he was playing a trick on me and deliberately going out of the way to extend the time. The situation was similar to that in a nation when the government, for a special reason, does something extraordinary which the people do not understand, and the people misinterpret it and find fault. But that chauffeur, going by the route he had chosen, reached Hongkow in not over fifteen minutes. My indignation cooled and I asked the chauffeur why he had come by such a circuitous route. He replied, "If we had taken the direct route, we would have driven

分鐘之內，可以不可以趕到虹口」？那個車夫答應說：「一定可以趕到」。我便坐上車，由車夫自由去駕駛，向目的地出發。上海的道路，我是很熟悉的，由法國租界開到虹口，好比由廣州沙基到東山一樣，一定要經過長堤和川龍口，才是捷徑。但是我的汽車夫從開車以後，所走的路，便不經過長堤和川龍口，他先由豐寧路再繞道德宣路，走小北門然後才到大東門，才抵東山。當時汽車走的飛快，聲音很大，我不能够和車夫說話，心裏便很奇怪，便非常的恨那個車夫，以爲車夫和我搗亂，是故意的走彎曲路阻遲時候。此時的情形，好比是政府有特別原故，要做非常的事，國民不知道，便生出許多誤會來非難政府一樣。至於那個車夫選擇那一條路走，不過十五分鐘便到了虹口，我的忿氣才平，便問那個車夫說：「爲甚麼要這樣彎彎曲曲走一條路呢」？那個車夫答應說：「如果走直路，便要經過大馬路，大馬路

110

along the Nanking Road where traffic is heavy with street cars, automobiles, jinrickshas, pedestrains, and moving vans, and where it is difficult to get through." This cleared up my misunderstanding; I realized that the way I had planned through Nanking Road and over the Garden Bridge at the Bund was conceived only in terms of distance, but the chauffeur had experience. He knew that an automobile could travel very fast, thirty or forty miles an hour, and that a few more turns and a few more miles with the chance, however, of increasing the speed, would still put us at our destination within the appointed time. He calculated directly from the time; he was not a philosopher and did not understand the formal relations of time and space, but he was a specialist in his line. He knew that an automobile has the power of shortening distance, and that if he could increase the speed of the car a few more turns would not prevent him from reaching Hongkow within fifteen minutes. If I had not given the chauffeur complete authority and allowed him freedom of movement, but had insisted that he take my route, I certainly could not have kept my engagement. Because I trusted him as an expert and did not bind his arm, he was able to take that route

的電車汽車人力車和行人貨物的來往是很擁擠的，是很不容易走通的」。我才明白從前誤會的道理，才曉得我所要走的大馬路外擺渡橋是從空間着想，那個車夫是有經驗的，知道汽車能够走得很快。每小時可以走三四十英里，雖然走彎一點，多走幾里路，但是把汽車的速度加快一點，還是在限定鐘點以內可以趕到。他的這樣打算，是從時間上着想。那個車夫不是哲學家，本不知道用甚麼時間空間去打算，不過他是專門家，知道汽車有縮地的能力，如果把汽車的速度加快，就是多走彎路，還能够於十五分鐘之內趕到虹口。假若當時我不給車夫以全權，由他自由去走，要依我的走法，一定是趕不到。因為我信他是專門家，不掣他的肘，他要走那一條路便走那一條路，所以能够在預約時間之內，可以趕到。不過我不是這種專門家，所以當時那個車夫走彎路，我便發生誤會，便不知道他何以要走彎路的道理。民國的

111

which he thought was best, and arrived at the appointed time. But since I was not an expert, I misunderstood why he should go out of the direct way. The people are masters of the nation and should act towards the government as I did towards the chauffeur on that ride to Hongkow, that is, let it drive and choose the way. Only such a conception of government will change the attitude of people towards government.

The hostility of Western peoples towards their governments is due to their failure to separate sovereignty from ability, and consequently they have not yet cleared up the difficulties of democracy. Let us not, as we pursue democracy, copy the West; let us make a clear distinction between sovereignty and ability. Although the democratic ideas came to us from Europe and America, yet the administration of democracy has not been successfully worked out there. We know a way now to make use of democracy and we know how to change the attitude of people towards government, but yet the majority of the people are without vision. We who have prevision must lead them and guide them into the right way if we want to escape the confusions of Western democracy and not follow in the tracks of the West. Western

人民都是國家的主人，對於政府的態度，應該要學我那次到虹口對車夫的態度一樣，把他當作是走路的車夫。能夠有這樣的眼光，人民對於政府的態度，才可以改變。

歐美人民現在對於政府，持反對的態度，是因為權與能沒有分開，所以民權的問題至今不能解決。我們實行民權，便不要學歐美，要把權與能分得清清楚楚。民權思想，雖然是由歐美傳進來的，但是歐美的民權問題，至今還沒有辦法。我們現在已經想出了辦法，知道人民要怎麼樣，才對於政府可以改變態度。但是人民都是不知不覺的多，我們先知先覺的人，便要為他們指導，引他們上軌道去走，那才能避了歐美的紛亂，不蹈歐美的覆轍。歐美學者現在只研究到了人民對於政府的態度不對，應該要改變。但是用甚麼

scholars to-day have only gotten to the point of realizing that the attitude of the people towards government is wrong and ought to be changed, but they do not yet see how to change it. I have now discovered the way—we must distinguish between sovereignty and ability. The foundation of the government of a nation must be built upon the rights of the people, but the administration of government must be intrusted to experts. We must not look upon these experts as stately and grand presidents and ministers, but simply as our chauffeurs, as guards at the gate, as cooks, physicians, carpenters, or tailors. It does not matter what sort of workmen the people consider them. As long as they have this general attitude towards them, the state can be governed and the nation can go forward.

方法來改變。他們還沒有想到。我現在把這個方法已經發明了,這個方法是要權與能分開。講到國家的政治,根本上要人民有權,至於管理政府的人,便要付之於有能的專門家。把那些專門家不要看作是很榮耀很尊貴的總統總長,只把他們當作是開汽車的車夫,或者是當作看門的巡捕,或者是弄飯的廚子,或者是診病的醫生,或者是做屋的木匠,或者是做衣的裁縫,無論把他們看作那一種的工人,都是可以的。人民要有這樣的態度,國家才有辦法,才能夠進步。

# LECTURE SIX*

## 第 六 講

民國十三年四月二十六日講

WESTERN statesmen and students of jurisprudence now speak of government as machinery and of law as an instrument. A great many Chinese books on government and law are translations from the Japanese; the Japanese have given government organization the designation of *chi-kuan* (organ, or bureau). *Chi-kuan* means the same thing as the common word "machinery" in China; when we say *chi-kuan* we mean the same thing as machinery, an administrative organ may, therefore, be called administrative machinery. But what is the difference between political machinery and manufacturing machinery? Manufacturing machinery is made entirely of material things—wood, steel, leather belts, and such—fitted together; political machinery is constructed of human beings and depends upon human beings, not material things, for its action. So there are great differences between political and manufacturing machinery, but the

現在歐美的政治家同法律學者,都說政府是機器,法律是機器之中的工具。中國很多的政治法律書籍,都是從日本譯過來的,日本人把政治組織,譯作機關,這個機關的意思,就是中國人所常說的機器一樣。因為機關和機器的意思相同,所以行政機關,就可以說是行政機器。至於行政機器和製造機器,有甚麼分別呢?製造機器,完全是用物質做成的,譬如用木料鋼鐵和皮帶種種東西,湊合起來,便做成製造機器。行政機器,完全是用人組織成的,種種動作,都是靠人去活動,不是靠物去活動。所以行政機器和製造機器,有大大的分別。最要緊的分別,就是行政機器,是靠人的能力去發動的,製造機器,

* Delivered on April 26, 1924.

114

one that stands out is the fact that political machinery is moved by human forces, while manufacturing machinery is moved by material forces.

Western civilization and culture have been developing and progressing with great rapidity. But when we analyze this progress we find that material civilization, as represented by manufacturing machinery, has been advancing very rapidly, while human machinery, as seen in political organization, has made very slow advance. What is the reason for this? When material machinery is constructed, it can be easily tried out, the bad features can be discarded, and the imperfect parts can be improved. But after human machinery has been set up, it is not easily experimented with and improvements are not at all easily made, except through revolution. The only other way would be to treat it as scrap iron, as we do old material machinery, but this is manifestly impossible. Hence manufacturing machinery in the West has progressed by leaps and bounds, while political machinery has just stumbled along. There is nothing over ten years old among the machines used in modern agriculture, industry, and business; for every decade brings numerous inventions and improvements and

是靠物的能力去發動的。

近來的歐美文化，是很發達的，文明是很進步的。分析起來說，他們的物質文明，像製造機器那些東西的進步，是很快的，至於人為機器，像政府機關這些東西的進步，是很慢的。這個理由，是在甚麼地方呢？就是物質機器做成了之後，易於試驗，試驗之後，不好的易於放棄，不備的易於改良。人為機器成立了之後，很不容易試驗，試驗之後，很不容易改良。假若是要改良，除非起革命不可。如果不然，要把他當作不好的物質機器看待，變成廢鐵，那是做不來的。因為這個理由，所以歐美的製造機器，進步很快，行政機器，進步很慢。現在農工商業中所有的機器，沒有十年以前的舊東西。因為每過十年，便有很多的新發明，很多的改良，沒有那一年不是有進步的。說到一百多年以前的行政機

every year marks some advance. Yet the political machinery of a hundred years ago is still in use to-day. The individual human beings in this machinery of human forces can change at will, but the whole organization is not easily reconstructed from the bottom up because of deep-seated habits and the close sequence of life activities. Without some sort of revolution, it is impossible in ordinary times to discard entirely the old organization. This explains the rapid advance of material machinery in the West, while political machinery advanced so slowly and with such difficulty.

In two former lectures, I said that Westerners had not yet found a fundamental method of procedure in carrying out democratic government. This is because they have not experimented carefully and skillfuly with their political machinery. Between the first inventions of material machinery and the machinery we see to-day there have been we know not how many thousands of experiments and improvements. This led to our modern automatic machines. The machinery of democratic government, after more than a hundred years, is limited to the power of voting; there has been no advance beyond this stage for a long time. There is no other way of controlling

關，至今還是應用他，這便是由於用人活動的機關，當中活動的人，固然可以隨時改換，但是全體組織，不容易根本改造。因爲習慣太久，陳陳相因，如果不想革命，要在平時去改造，把舊組織完全廢棄，那是做不到的。由於這個道理，歐美的物質機器，近來很容易進步，。進步是很快的，人爲機器，向來便難於進步，進步是很慢的。

我在前兩次講演民權，便說歐美對於民權政治，至今沒有根本辦法。他們爲甚麼沒有辦法呢？就是因爲他們把人爲的機器，沒有精良去試驗。說到物質的機器，自最初發明時代，以至於現在，不知道古人經過了幾千次的試驗，和幾千次的改良，才有今日我們所見的機器。民權政治的機器，至今有了一百多年，沒有改變。我們拿現在民權政治的機器來看，各國所行的民權，只有一個選舉權。從有了選舉權以後，許久都沒有別的

the men who are elected to office, whether they turn out to be worthy or incompetent. Such a condition is due to imperfections in the machinery of democracy, and consequently democratic government has not yet found a good mode of procedure and has made but little progress. If we want to improve the machinery, what shall we do? As I said in my previous lecture, we must make a clear distinction between sovereignty and ability.

Statesmen and students of jurisprudence are now speaking of government as a machine and of law as an instrument, and our modern democratic age looks upon the people as the motive power in government. In the old autocratic age the king was the motive power and all the activities of the state were initiated by him. The greater the power of the government, the greater the majesty of the throne. A strong government was essential for the effective carrying out of the imperial edicts. Since the king was the power behind the machinery, a s t r o n g government organization made it possible for the king, in his exalted position, to do whatever he pleased—initiate political reforms, carry on "long-range aggressions," prepare for war, or anything else. So in the age of autocracy, increased power in the government brought

進步。選舉出來的人，究竟是賢與不肖，便沒有別的權去管他，像這種情形，就是民權政治的機器不完全。因爲這種機器不完全，所以民權政治，至今還沒有好辦法，還沒有大進步。我們要這種機器進步，是從甚麼地方做起呢？照前一次所講的道理，是要把權和能分清楚。

現在的政治家和法律學者，都以政府爲機器，以法律爲工具。此刻的民權時代，是以人民爲動力，從前的君權時代，是以皇帝爲動力，全國的動作，是發源於皇帝。在那個時代，政府的力量越大，皇帝越顯尊嚴，有了强有力的政府，皇帝的號令才容易實行，因爲皇帝是發動機器的人，所以政府的力越大，皇帝高高在上，便可以爲所欲爲。譬如修內治，勤遠略，整軍經武，他要想做甚麼，便可以做甚麼，故在君權時代，政府的力越大，對於皇帝，只有利而無害。到了民權時代，人民就是政府的原動力，爲甚麼人民不

advantage but no injury to the king. But in the age of democracy, people are the motive power in government. Then why are they loath to have too strong a government? Because if the government is too powerful they cannot control it and will be oppressed by it. Because they were once excessively oppressed by their government and suffered so much from it, they are trying to prevent oppression in the future by limiting the power of government. These are the early days of democracy and our methods of controlling government are also defective. The people are naturally the motive power in a democracy, but the people must also be able at any time to recall the power they set loose. Therefore the people will use only a low-powered government, for they cannot control a government of several hundred thousand horse power and will not dare to use it. The fear of powerful government among Western peoples to-day is just like the fear of powerful machinery in the old factories. As for their political machinery, however, the people are not thinking of ways to improve it and are fearful of giving it too much power lest they be unable to call the power back. Instead, they are constantly thinking of ways to limit the government until it has no

118

願意政府的能力太大呢？因為政府的力量過大，人民便不能管理政府，要被政府來壓迫。從前被政府的壓迫太過。所受的痛苦太多，現在要免去那種壓迫的痛苦，所以不能不防止政府的能力。現在是民權初發達的時代，管理政府的方法也是不完全。政府的動力，固然是發源於人民，但是人民發出了動力之後，還要隨時可以收回來，像那樣小力的政府，人民才是敢用他。若是有了幾萬匹馬力的政府，人民不能夠管理，便不敢用他。所以現在歐美各國的人民，恐怕強有的政府，好比從前的工廠，怕有大馬力的機器是一樣的道理。至於政治的機器，人民總不知道想方法來改良，總是怕政府的能力太大，不能拉回，反常常想方法去防止，所以弄到政治不能發達，民權沒有進步。照現在世界的潮流說，民權思想是一天一天的進步，管理民權政治的機器，還絲毫沒有進步。所

chance to develop and democracy has no chance to advance. Looking at present tendencies in the world, we may say that there is steady progress in democratic ideas but no progress at all in the control of democratic government. This is the reason why Western democratic nations have not found as yet a fundamental method of procedure.

As I have said in my preceding lecture, we must make a distinction between sovereignty and ability. When we apply this distinction to the illustsration of the machine, where do we place the ability or power? The machine itself is what possesses the ability or power. A 100,000 horse power machine, fed with the proper amount of coal and water, will generate the proper ability and power. Where is the sovereignty? The engineer in control of the machine possesses the sovereignty. No matter what the horse power of the machine, the engineer has only to move his hand and machine will start and start immediately, or stop and stop immediately. The engineer can control the machine, and make it do as he wishes; as soon as the machine starts he can make the steamship or the train go very fast, and by stopping the machine he can make the steamer or the train cease moving. The machine, then,

以歐美的民權政治,至今沒有根本辦法,就是這個理由。

照我前一次所講的根本辦法說,權與能要分別清楚,用機器來做比喻,甚麼是有能力的東西呢?機器的本體,就是有能力的東西。譬如十萬匹馬力的機器,供給了相當的煤和水之後,便可以發生相當的能力。甚麼是有權的人呢?管理機器的工程師就是有權的人。無論機器是有多少馬力,只要工程師一動手,要機器開動便立刻開動,要機器停止,便立刻停止。工程師管理機器,想要怎麼樣,便可以怎麼樣。好像輪船火車,一開機器,便可以要輪船火車走得很快,一停機器,馬上就可以要他不走。所以機器是很有能的東西,工程師是很有權的人。人民管理政府,如果把權和能分開了,

119

is an able and powerful thing, while the engineer is a man with a large degree of sovereignty. If the people in their control of government will make a distinction between sovereignty and ability or power, they will be like the engineer who controls the great machinery. When democracy is highly developed and methods of controling government are perfected, the government will have great power, but the people will only have to make their opinions known in their national congress; if they attack the government, they may overthrow it, or if they laud the government they may strengthen it. But as it is, if the government carries on with a high hand, the people have no way to control it; no matter how much the people may criticize or praise the government, their words are ineffective and the government pays no attention to them. To-day government is making no progress, while the democratic spirit flourishes. The people of all countries are finding that the present political machinery does not suit their ideas or needs.

China now is in a period of revolution. We are advocating a democratic form of government. Our ideas of democracy have come from the West. We have recently been thinking how we might copy

也要像工程師管理機器一樣。在民權極盛的時代，管理政府的方法很完全，政府就是有大力，人民只要把自己的意見，在國民大會上去發表，對於政府加以攻擊，便可以推翻，對政府加以頌揚，便可以鞏固。但是現在的權與能不分，政府過於專橫，人民沒有方法來管理，不管人民是怎麼樣攻擊，怎麼樣頌揚，政府總是不理，總是不能發生效力。現在世界上的政治不進步，民權思想很發達，無論那一國的人民，對於政治機器的現狀，總是不合他們心理上的用法。

中國此刻正是改革時代，我們對於政治，主張實行民權，這種民權思想，是由歐美傳進來的。我們近來想學歐美的新思想，造成一個

these ideas and build up a nation under popular government. When we were first considering this kind of state, one group of revolutionary enthusiasts believed that if we would imitate the West exactly, follow right in the tracks of the West, and copy everything from the West, then Chinese democracy would develop to the limit of perfection. At first such ideas were not entirely wrong, for China's old autocratic government was so corrupt that if we could, after effecting a revolution and overthrowing the autocracy, begin our constructive effort by learning from the West, we should certainly be better off than under the old regime. But are the peoples of the West thoroughly satisfied with the present situation in their national and social life? If we will make a careful study of Western government and society we shall find that in the so-called pioneer revolutionary states, like the United States and France, people are still proposing improvements in government and are still thinking of revolution. Why, when they had revolutions a century ago, are they thinking of other revolutions? This proves that we were wrong when we thought that following the West would lead us to the heights of perfection; and if we should fully copy the United States

完全的民治國家。最初想造成這種國家的時候，一般革命志士，都以為完全仿傚歐美，步歐美的後塵，把歐美的東西完全抄過來，中國的民權，便算是很發達，便可以算是止境。當初的這種思想，並不是全錯，因為中國從前的專制政體，過於腐敗，我們如果實行改革，打破了專制以後，做建設的事業，能夠學到像歐美，就比較上說當然是很好。但是歐美人民對於自己國家社會的現狀是不是心滿意足呢？如果我們細心考察歐美的政治社會，所謂革命的先進國家，像美國法國的人民，現在還是主張改良政治，還是想要再來革命。他們革命，不過一百多年，為甚麼還要再來革命呢？由此便可以證明我們從前以為學到了像歐美，便算是止境，那便是不對。由此便知就令是我們學到了像美國法國一樣，法國美國現在還是要革命，我們到了百十年之後，一定也是免不了再起革命的。因為法國美國現在的政治機器，還是有

and France, which are still contemplating revolution, we could not escape another revolution a hundred years hence. For the governmental machinery of the United States and France still has many defects, and does not satisfy the desires of the people nor give them a complete measure of happiness. So we in our proposed reconstruction must not think that if we imitate the West of to-day we shall reach the last stage of progress and be perfectly contented. If we follow the dust of the West, will not each generation be more dissatisfied than the one previous, and will we not finally have to stage another revolution? If another revolution is going to be necessary, then is not this one a vain effort? What shall we do to keep this revolution from being a futile waste of energy? What plans shall we lay in order to secure a permanent government and a lasting peace—"enduring repose after one supreme effort"—and prevent calamities in the future?

Can we bring over the methods of the West and apply them wholesale in China?

As I said in a former lecture, Europe and America have not gone to the bottom in their study of the problems of democracy, and consequently the people are in daily conflict with their governments.

很多的缺點，還是不能滿足人民的慾望，人民還是不能享圓滿的幸福。像這樣講來，所以我們現在提倡改革，決不能夠說學到了像現在的歐美，便算是止境，便以爲心滿意足。我們步他們的後塵，豈不是一代更不如一代，還再要起革命嗎？若是再起革命，那麼此次的革命豈不是徒勞無功嗎？我們要現在的革命不是徒勞無功，想存一個長治久安之計，所謂一勞永逸，免將來的後患，要怎麼樣才可以做得到呢？

歐美的方法，可不可以完全搬到中國來行呢？

我在前一次講過了，歐美對於民權問題的研究，還沒有澈底。因爲不澈底，所以人民和政府，日日相衝突。因爲民權是新力量，政府

122

The force of democracy is new, but the machinery of democracy is old. If we want to solve the difficulties of democracy we must build another machinery, a new machinery, upon the principle that sovereignty and ability are different things. The people must have sovereignty, the machinery must have ability and power. Modern efficient and powerful machinery is operated by men who can start and stop it at will. The West has made the most complete inventions in the field of machinery but very imperfect discoveries in the field of government. If we want to make a complete change in government, we have no model to follow but must discover a new way for ourselves. Are we able to do such a thing? Since the Boxer year, Chinese have completely lost their self-confidence. The attitude of the people is one of absolute faith in foreign countries and distrust of themselves. That they should accomplish anything of themselves or make any original discovery seems to them impossible. No, they must run after the West and copy Western ways. We do not see that Western civilization is strong only in its material aspects and not in its various political aspects. From the standpoint of scientific theories of a material civilization, Europe and America

是舊機器，我們現在要解決民權問題，便要另造一架新機器。造成這種新機器的原理，是要分開權和能，人民是要有權的，權器是要有能的。現在有大能的新機器，用人去管理，要開動就開動，要停止就停止。這是由於歐美對於機器，有很完全的發明。但是他們對於政治，還是沒有很完全的發明。我們現在要有很完全的改革，無從學起，便要自己想出一個新辦法。要我們自己想出一個新辦法，可不可以做得到呢？中國人從經過了義和團之後，完全失掉了自信力。一般人的心理，總是信仰外國，不敢信仰自己，無論甚麼事，以為要自己去做成，單獨來發明，是不可能的，一定要步歐美的後塵，要倣效歐美的辦法。殊不知歐美的文明，只在物質的一方面，不在其他的政治各方面。專就物質文明的科學說，歐美近來本是很發達的。一個人對於一種學問，固然是有特長，但是對於其餘的各科學問，未必都是很精通的

have developed remarkably in recent years. But because a man is standing in one field of knowledge does not necessarily signify that he is equally proficient in all fields of knowledge; in many of them he may even be blind. Their physical sciences have developed to the highest point in the past century and their many new inventions have "usurped the powers of Nature" beyond our wildest dreams. But to say that what they have not thought of in political science we cannot think of or discover is unreasonable. Western machinery has indeed made much progress in recent times, but this does not prove that Western political systems have progressed also. For two or more centuries the specialty of the West has been only science. The great scientists are naturally well advanced in their own branches of knowledge, but this does not necessarily make them equally advanced in all branches of knowledge.

Western science has progressed to the point of making material machinery automatically double-acting but the people's sovereignty over the government is still single-acting; it can only be advanced and not taken back. While we are advocating democracy for the reconstruction of our republic, let us have a thoroughgoing new democ-

○還有許多都是盲然的○他們的物質科學，一百多年以來，發明到了極點，許多新發明眞是巧奪天工，是我們夢想不到的○如果說政治學問，他們從前沒有想到的，我們現在也想不到，那便是沒有理由○歐美的機器，近來本有很完全的進步，但是不能說他們的機器是進步，政治也是進步○因爲近兩百多年以來，歐美的特長只有科學，大科學家對於本行的學問，固然是有專長，對於其餘的學問，像政治哲學等，未必就有兼長○

歐美科學在近幾十年以來，本來是進步到了極點，所以做出來的物質機器，有往返的兩面動力，來回可以自動，但是做成的政治機器，還只有一面的動力，人民對於政府的權力，只能夠發出去，不能夠

racy and a thoroughgoing new republic. If we should not wholly follow the advanced states of the West, we should think out a new and better procedure ourselves. Are we capable of doing this? For thousands of years China has been an independent country. In our former political development, we never borrowed materials from other countries. China had one of the earliest civilizations in the world and never needed to copy wholly from others. Only in recent times has Western culture advanced beyond ours, and the passion for this new civilization has stimulated our revolution. Now that the revolution is a reality, we naturally desire to see China excel the West and build up the newest and most progressive state in the world. We certainly possess the qualifications necessary to reach this ideal, but we must not merely imitate the democratic systems of the West. These systems have become old-style machinery.

To reach our ideal we must construct a new machinery. Is there any material in the world for such a new machinery? Yes, there is much material scattered in various countries, but we must first decide upon a fundamental line of procedure. And this line of procedure is the separation of sovereignty and ability which I have already dis-

收回來。我們現在主張民權，來改造民國，將來造成的新民國，一定是要澈底，要造成澈底的新民國，在歐美的先進國家，無從完全傲效，我們自己便要另想一個新辦法。這種新辦法，歐美還沒有完全想到，我們能不能夠想到呢？中國幾千年以來，都是獨立國家，從前政治的發達，向來沒有假借外國材料的。中國在世界之中，文化上是先進的國家，外國的材料，向來無可完全傲效。歐美近來的文化，才比中國進步。我們羨慕他們的新文明，才主張革命，此刻實行革命，當然是要中國駕乎歐美之上，改造成世界上最新最進步的國家。我們要達到這種目的，實在是有這種資格，不過歐美現在的民權政府，還是不完全傲效，他們的政府，已經成了舊機器。

我們要另外造出一架新機器，才可以達到我們的目的。此刻想要造出一架新機器，世界上有沒有新材料呢？現在散在各國的新材料是很多的，不過要先定一個根本辦法。我在前一次所主張的分開權與能，便是這一種的根本辦法。根本辦法定了之後

cussed. Then, as we put democracy into operation, we must separate the organization of the state and the administration of democracy. Western nations have not thought through these basic principles and have not distinguished between sovereignty and power or ability, consequently their government's power does not expand. Now that we have thought through our basic principle, we must go a step further and divide the machinery of government. In order to do this, we must understand well the idea of government. In Lecture One, I gave a definition for government—a thing of and by all the people and control of the affairs of all the people. The government machinery which is constructed according to the principle of sovereignty being distinct from ability and power is just like material machinery which has power in itself and is controlled by a power outside. In building the new state according to the newest discoveries, we should separate clearly these two kinds of power. But how? We must start from the meaning of government. Government or politics is a concern of all the people, and its centralizing force is political sovereignty. Political sovereignty, then, means popular sovereignty, and government which centralizes

，去實行民權，還要分開國家的組織與民權的行使。歐美的根本辦法，沒有想通，不能分開權與能，所以政府能力不能擴充，我們的根本辦法已經想通了，更進一步，就是分開政治的機器。要分開政治的機器，先要明白政治的意義。政是衆人之事，治是管理衆人之事。現在分開權與能，所造成的政治機器，就是像物質的機器一樣，其中有機器本體的力量，有管理機器的力量，現在用新發明來造新國家，就要把這兩種力量分別清楚。要怎麼樣才可以分別清楚呢？根本上還是要再從政治的意義來研究，政是衆人之事，集合衆人之事的大力量，便叫做政權，政權就可以說是民權。治是管理衆人之事，集合管理衆人之事的大力量，便叫做治權，治權就可以說是政府權。

the forces controlling the life of the people is called government power or government authority.

There are, then, two forces in politics, the political power of the people and the administrative power of the government. One is the power of control, the other is the power of the government itself. What does this mean? A steamship has a 100,000 horse power engine: the generation of 100,000 horse power and the moving of the vessel are in the power of the machinery itself, and this power may be compared to the power of the government. But the movement of the great steam vessel forward and backward, to the right or left, its stopping, and its rate of speed, all depend upon the control of a good engineer. He is essential to the direction and control of a perfect machine; by perfect control the powerful vessel can be made to start and to stop at will. This power of control may be compared to the control over government, which is political sovereignty. Building a new state is like building a new steamship. If we put in low-power-ed machinery, the speed of the vessel will naturally be low, its

所以政治之中，包含有兩個力量，一個是政權，一個是治權。這兩個力量，一個是管理政府的力量，一個是政府自身的力量。這是甚麼意思呢？好比有十萬匹馬力的輪船機器，那架機器能夠發生十萬匹馬力，來運動輪船，這便是機器本體的力量。這種力量，就好比是政府自身的力量一樣，這種自身的力量，就是治權。至於這樣大的輪船，或者是要前進，或者是要後退，或者是要向左右轉，或者是要停止，以及所走的速度，或者是要快，或者是要慢，更要有很好的工程師，用很完全的機器，才可以駕駛，才可以管理。有了很完全的駕駛管理之力量，才可以令那樣大力的輪船，要怎麼樣開動，便是怎麼樣開動，要怎麼樣停止，便是怎麼樣停止。這種開動停止的力量，便是管理輪船的力量，這種力量，就好比是管理政府的力量一樣。這種管理的大力量，就是政權。我們造新國家，好比是造新輪船一樣，船中所裝的機器，如果所發生的馬力很小，行船的速

127

freight capacity will be small, and profits from its running meager. But if we install high-powered machinery, the vessel will have a high rate of speed, will be able to carry heavy freight and will bring in large profits. If we could build a steamship with a speed of 50 knots, then no other steamship could compete with it, and we would have the fastest and largest new steamship in the world. The same principle applies in the building of a state. If we construct a lowpowered, weak government, its activities will be limited and its accomplishments will be meager. But if we put in a highpowered, strong government, its activities will be broad in scope and it will accomplish great things. If a powerful government should be installed in the largest state in the world, would not that state outstrip all others? Would not that government be unequaled under heaven?

Why have the nations of the West steamships with high-powered machinery but not states with highpowered strong governments? Because they can only control highpowered machinery, but have not found a way to control high-powered government. To discard a low-

度當然是很慢，所載的貨物當然很少，所收的利息當然是很微。反過來說，如果所發生的馬力很大，行船的速度當然是極快，所載的貨物當然是極多，所收的利息也當然是極大。如果我們所造的新輪船，每小時可以走五十海里，世界上便沒有別的輪船能夠來比賽。我們的輪船，就是世界上最快最大的新輪船。創造國家，也是一樣的道理。如果在國家之內，所建設的政府，只要他發生很小的力量，是沒有力的政府，那麼這個政府，所做的事業，當然是很小，所成就的功效當然是很微。若是要他發生很大的力量，是強有力的政府，那麼這個政府，所做的事業當然是很大，所成就的功效也當然是極大。假設在世界上的最大國家之內建設一個極強有力的政府，那麼這個國家，豈不是駕乎各國之上的國家，這個政府豈不是無敵於天下的政府？

歐美到了今日，為甚麼還是只造有大馬力的機器之輪船，不造極強有力的政府之國家呢？因為他們現在的人民，只有方法來管理大馬力的機器，沒有方法來管理強有力的政府，而

powered old vessel and build a high-powered new one is an easy task; but the state has very deep roots and the construction of a new powerful government in place of an old weak government is a very difficult thing. China with her four hundred million people is the most populous state in the world; her territory is broad and her products are rich and abundant, exceeding those of the United States. The United States has now become the wealthiest and most powerful nation in the world, and no other nation can compare with her. When we compare our natural resources, it seems that China should outstrip the United States, but as a matter of fact, not only is this impossible now but the two countries cannot even be mentioned in the same breath. The reason is that the Chinese have the necessary qualifications but want human effort. We have never had a real good government. But if we add human effort to our natural qualifications, build up a complete, strong government which will display great power and move the whole nation, then China can immediately begin to advance in line with the United States.

After China secures a powerful government, we must not be afraid, as Western peoples are, that the government will become too strong

且不要小馬力的舊船，另外造一隻大馬力的新船，是很容易的事。至於國家，已經是根深蒂固。有了沒有力的舊政府，要另外造成一個強有力的新政府，那是很不容易的事。說到我們中國人口，有了四萬萬，是世界上人口最多的國家，領土寬濶，物產豐富，都要在美國之上。美國成了現在世界上最富最強的國家，沒有那一國可以和他並駕齊驅，就天然的富源來比較，中國還應該要駕乎美國之上。但是現在的實情，不但是不能駕乎美國之上，並且不能夠和美國相提並論。此中原因，就是我們中國只有天然的資格，缺少人為的工夫，從來沒有很好的政府。如果用這種天然的資格，再加以人為的工夫，建設一個很完全很有力的政府。發生極大力量，運動全國，中國便可以和美國馬上並駕齊驅。

中國有了強有力的政府之後，我們便不要像歐美的人民，怕政府的力量太大不能夠管理

and out of control. Because our plan
for the reconstructed state includes
the division of the political power
of the whole state into two parts.
The political power will be given
into the hands of the people, who
will have a full degree of sovereignty and will be able to control
directly the affairs of state; this
political power is popular sovereignty. The other power is government, and we will put that entirely
in the government organs, which
will be powerful and will manage
all the nation's business; this
political power is the power of
government. If the people have a
full measure of political sovereignty
and the methods for exercising
popular control over the government are well worked out, we need
not fear that the government will
become too powerful and uncontrollable. Westerners formerly did
not dare to build machines with
over 100,000 horse power; because
machines were not perfectly constructed and the means of control
were not compact, they were afraid
of their power and would not risk
the control of them. But now such
wonderful improvements have been
made in machinery, the machines
themselves are so well constructed
and the control mechanism is so
compact, that Westerners are
building machines with tremendous

130

○因為在我們的計劃之
中，想造成的新國家，
是要把國家的政治大權
分開成兩個：一個是政
權，要把這個大權，完
全交到人民的手內，要
人民有充分的政權，可
以直接去管理國事，這
個政權，便是民權。一
個是治權，要把這個大
權，完全交到政府的機
關之內，要政府有很大
的力量，治理全國事務
○這個治權，便是政府
權。人民有了很充分的
政權，管理政府的方法
很完全，便不怕政府的
力量太大，不能夠管理
○歐美從前不敢造十萬
匹馬力以上的機器，只
敢造十萬匹馬力以下的
機器，就是因為機器的
構造不完全，管理的方
法不周密，所以便怕機
器的力量太大，不敢管
理○到了現在，機器很
進步，機器本體的構造
，既是很完全，管理機
器的方法，又是很周密
，所以便造極大馬力的
機器○我們要造政治的
機器，要政治的機器進
步，也是要跟這一樣的
路走，要有構造很完全
和有大力的政府機關，
同時又要有管理這個機

horse power. If we want to build a much-improved political machinery, we must follow the same line: we must have a complete and powerful government organ, and at the same time have a compact method of popular sovereignty to exercise control over the government organ. Western governments lack this compact and effective control, so they are not yet making much progress. Let us not follow in their tracks. Let the people in thinking about government distinguish between sovereignty and power. Let the great political force of the state be divided; first let there be the power of the government and then the power of the people. Such a division will make the government the machinery and the people the engineer. The attitude of the people towards their government will then be like the attitude of the engineer towards his machinery.

Such advances have been made in the construction of machinery that not only men with mechanical knowledge, but even children without any knowledge of machinery can control it.

China has now the idea of democracy, but no perfect machinery has yet been invented in the world to express this idea. The people

關很周密的方法。歐美對於政府，因為沒有管理很周密的方法，所以他們的政治機關，至今還是不發達。我們要不蹈他們的覆轍，根本上要人民對於政府的態度，分開權與能，把政治的大權分開成兩個：一個是政府權，一個是人民權。像這樣的分開，就是把政府當作機器，把人民當作工程師，人民對於政府的態度，就好比是工程師，對於機器一樣。

現在機器的構造很進步，不但是有機器知識的人，可以來管理，就是沒有機器知識的小孩子，也是可以來管理。

現在中國有了民權的思想，但是關於這種思想的機器，世界上還沒有發明完全，一般人

131

do not know how to use it. We who have vision and foresight must first build the machine. We must construct a very serviceable kind of faucet, a very safe kind of electric button which ordinary people can learn how to use by a single turn of the hand; then the idea of democracy will become a reality. What methods shall we use in applying the democracy which we have adopted from the West? Only after we have thought through these methods will democracy be adapted to our use. If we insist on using democracy without careful preparation beforehand, we will find it extremely dangerous and liable to kill us. Have such methods of applying democracy yet been found? Switzerland in Europe has some partial methods which she has already tried out; they are radical and give the people direct sovereignty, but are not very complete. The larger nations of Europe have not even experimented with these incomplete methods. The fact that only the small state of Switzerland has tried a partial form of direct sovereignty makes many people question whether it is applicable in large states also. Why are not the large states using Switzerland's methods? Because they "fear difficulties and seek ease," these advanced people, though familiar

民都不知道用他，我們先知先覺的人，便應該先來造好這種機器，做一個很便利的放水制，做一個很安全的接電鈕，只要普通人一轉手之勞，便知道用他，然後才可以把這種思想，做成事實。中國人得到民權思想本是在歐美之後，好像築鐵路，是在日本之後一樣。至於我們在歐美之後，要想有甚麼方法，才可以來使用民權呢？這種方法想通了，民權才可以供我們的使用。若是這種方法沒有想通，民權便不能供我們的使用。如果一定要去使用，便是很危險，現在世界上有沒有這種方法呢？在歐洲有一個瑞士國，已經有了這幾部分的方法，已經試驗了這幾部分的方法，這是澈底的方法，是直接的民權，不過不大完全能了。至於歐洲的那些大國就是還不完全的方法，還是沒有試驗，因為試驗這幾部分之方法的國家，只有瑞士的一個小國，沒有別的大國，所以許多人便懷疑起來，說這幾部分的方法，只有在小國能夠使用，在大國不能夠用。歐洲的大國為甚麼不用這幾部分的方法呢？因為畏難苟安，注重經濟，所以他們的先進國

with the newly invented models, do not make use of them. But we in China never had any old machinery of democracy, so we ought to be able to choose and use the newest and best discoveries.

What are the newest discoveries in the way of applying democracy? First, there is the suffrage, and it is the only method in operation throughout the so-called modern democracies. Is this one form of popular sovereignty enough in government? This one power by itself may be compared to the early machines which could move forward only but not back. The second of the newly discovered methods is the power of recall. With this power, the people can pull the machine back. These two rights, the right to elect and the right to recall, give the people control over their officials and enable them to put all government officials in their positions or to move them out of their positions. The coming and going of officials follows the free will of the people just as modern machines move to and fro by the free action of the engine. Another important thing in a state, in addition to officials, is law; "with men to govern there must also be ways of governing." What power must the people possess in order to control the laws? If all the people think that a certain law

家，就是知道了這些新式發明，還是不採用他。說到我們中國，關於民權的機器，從前沒有舊東西，現在很可以採用最近最好的新發明。

關於民權一方面的方法，世界上有了一些甚麼最新式的發明呢？第一個是選舉權。現在世界上所謂先進的民權國家，普遍的祇實行這一個民權，專行這一個民權，在政治之中是不是夠用呢？專行這一個民權，好比是最初次的舊機器，只有把機器推到前進的力，沒有拉回來的力。現在新式的方法除了選舉權之外，第二個就是罷免權，人民有了這個權便有拉回來的力。這兩個權是管理官吏的，人民有了這兩個權，對於政府之中的一切官吏，一面可以放出去，又一面可以調回來，來去都可以從人民的自由。這好比是新式的機器，一推一拉，都可以由機器的自動。國家除了官吏之外，還有甚麼重要東西呢？其次的就是法律，所謂有了治人，還要有治法。人民要有甚麼權，才可以

would be of great advantage to them, they should have the power to decide upon this law and turn it over to the government for execution. This third kind of popular power is called the initiative. If everybody thinks that an old law is not beneficial to the people, they should have the power to amend it and to ask the government to administer the revised law and do away with the old law. This is called the referendum and is a fourth form of popular sovereignty. Only when the people have these four powers can we say that there is a full measure of democracy, and only where these four powers are effectively applied can we say that there is thoroughgoing, direct, popular sovereignty. Before there was any complete democracy, people elected their officials and representatives and then could not hold them responsible. This was only indirect democracy or a representative system of government. The people could not control the government directly but only through their representative. For direct control of the government it is necessary that the people practice these four forms of popular sovereignty. Only then can we speak of government by all the people. This means that our four hundred millions shall be king, exerting their kingly authority and

管理法律呢？如果大家看到了一種法律，以爲是很有利於人民的，便要有一種權，自己決定出來，交到政府去執行，關於這種權，叫做創制權，這就是第三個民權。若是大家看到了從前的舊法律，以爲是很不利於人民的，便要有一種權，自己去修改，修改好了之後，便要政府執行修改的新法律，廢止從前的舊法律，關於這種權，叫做複決權，這就是第四個民權。人民有了這四個權，才算是充分的民權，能够實行這四個權，才算是澈底的直接民權。從前沒有充分民權的時候，人民選舉了官吏議員之後，便不能够再問，這種民權。是間接民權。間接民權，就是代議政體，用代議士去管理政府，人民不能直接去管理政府。要人民能够直接管理政府，便要人民能够實行這四個民權。人民能够實行四個民權，才叫做全民政治。全民政治是甚麼意思呢？就是從前講過了的，用四萬萬人來做皇帝。四萬萬人要怎麼樣才可以

controlling the great affairs of state by means of the four powers of the people. These four powers are also called political powers and are powers for control of the government.

The government's own power to transact business may be called the power to work, to work on behalf of the people. If the people are very powerful, whether the government can work or not and what kind of work it does will depend entirely upon the will of the people. If the government is very powerful, as soon as it starts work it can display great strength, and whenever the people want it to stop, it will have to stop. In a nutshell, if the people are really to have direct control over the power of government they must be able to command at any time the actions of the government.

With the people exerting these four great powers to control the government, what methods will the government use in performing its work? In order that the government may have a complete organ through which to do its best work, there must be a quintuple-power constitution. A government is not complete and cannot do its work for the people unless it is based upon a quintuple-power constitution. I spoke before of an Ame-

做皇帝呢？就是要有這四個民權，來管理國家的大事。有了四個民權，便可以直接管理國家的政治。這四個民權，又叫做政權。

至於政府自己辦事的權，又可以說是做工權，就是政府來替人民做工夫的權。人民有了大權，政府能不能夠做工夫，要做甚麼樣的工夫，都要隨人民的志願。就是政府有了大權，一經發動做工夫之後，可以發生很大的力量，人民隨時要他停止，他便要停止。總而言之，要人民眞有直接管理政府之權，便要政府的動作，隨時受人民的指揮。

人民有了這四個大權，來管理政府，要政府去做工夫，在政府之中要用甚麼方法呢？要政府有很完全的機關，去做很好的工夫，便要用五權憲法。用五權憲法所組織的政府才是完全的政府，才是完全的政府機關。有了這種的政府機關，去替人民做工夫，才可以做很好很完全的工夫。從前說美

135

rican scholar who advanced the new theory that what a nation fears most is an all-powerful, uncontrollable government, yet what it most desires is an all-powerful government which the people can use and which will seek the people's welfare. Popular rule cannot really prevail until there is the latter kind of government. We are now making a distinction between sovereignty and ability; we are saying that the people are like the engineer and the government like the machinery. On the one hand, we want the government machinery to be all-powerful so that it can do any sort of work; on the other hand, we want the engineer-people to be very strong so that they can control the all-powerful machinery. Now what great powers are the people and the government each to have in order that they may balance each other? I have already discussed the four powers on the people's side —suffrage, recall, initiative, and referendum. On the side of the government there must be five powers —executive, legislative, judicial, civil service examination, and censoring. When the four political powers of the people control the five governing powers of the government, then we will have a completely democratic government organ, and the strength of the people and of

136

國有一位學者，對於政治學理上的最新發明，是說在一國之內，最怕的是有了一個萬能政府，人民不能管理，最希望的是要一個萬能政府，為人民使用，以謀人民的幸福。有了這種政府，民治才算是最發達。我們現在分開權與能，說人民是工程師，政府是機器，在一方面要政府的機器是萬能，無論甚麼事都可以做。又在他一方面要人民的工程師，也有大力量，可以管理萬能的機器，那麼在人民和政府的兩方面，彼此要有一些甚麼的大權，才可以彼此平衡呢？在人民一方面的大權，剛才已經講過了，是要有四個權。這四個權，是選舉權、罷免權、創制權、複決權。在政府一方面的，是要有五個權，這五個權，是行政權、立法權、司法權、考試權、監察權。用人民的四個政權，來管理政府的五個治權，那才算是一個完全的民權政治機關。有了這樣的政治機關，人民和政府的力量，才可以彼此平衡。我們要詳細明

the government will be well balanced. This diagram will help us to understand more clearly the relation between these powers:

POLITICAL POWER OF THE PEOPLE

| Suffrage | Recall | Initiative | Referendum |

ADMINISTRATIVE POWER OF
THE GOVERNMENT

| Legislature | Judiciary | Executive | Civil Service | Censorship Examinations |

The political power above is in the hands of the people, the administrative power below is in the hands of the government. The people control the government through the suffrage, the recall, the initiative, and the referendum; the government works for the people through its legislative, judicial, executive, civil examination, and censoring departments. With these nine powers in operation and preserving a balance, the problem of democracy will truly be solved and the government will have a definite course to follow. The materials for this new plan have been discovered before now. Switzerland has already applied three of the political powers but does not have the recall. Some of the northwestern states in

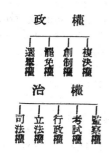

白這兩種大權的關係，可以用一個圖來說明。

政　權

選舉權　罷免權　創制權　複決權

治　權

司法權　立法權　行政權　考試權　監察權

就這個圖看，在上面的政權，就是人民權，在下面的治權，就是政府權。人民要怎麼樣管理政府，就是實行選舉權、罷免權、創制權和複決權。政府要怎麼樣替人民做工夫，就是實行行政權、立法權、司法權、考試權和監察權。有了這九個權，彼此保持平衡，民權問題才算是真解決，政治才算是有軌道。至於這九個權的材料，並不是今日發明的，譬如就政權說，在瑞士已經實行過了三個權，不過是沒有罷官權。在美國的西北幾省，現在除採用瑞士

137

the United States have taken over the three political rights from Switzerland and have added the right of recall. Suffrage is the people's power most widely exercised in the world to-day. Switzerland is already exercising three of the popular powers and one fourth of the United States is exercising all four. Where the four powers have been exercised in a careful, compact way the results have been excellent. They are facts of experience, not mere hypothetical ideals. We will be safe in using these methods and will not run into any danger.

All governmental powers were formerly monopolized by kings and emperors, but after the revolutions they were divided into three groups: thus the United States, after securing its independence, established a government with three coordinate departments, with splendid results. Other nations followed the example of the United States. But foreign governments have never exercised more than these three powers—legislative, executive, and judicial. What is the source of the two new features in our quintuple-power constitution? They come from old China. China long ago had the independent systems of civil service examination and censorship and

的三個政權以外，並加入一個罷免權。至於選舉權，更是世界上各國最通行的民權。所以就世界上民權的情形說，瑞士已經實行過了三權，美國有四分之一的省分，已經實行過了四權。他們在那幾部分的地方，實行這四個民權，有了很周密的辦法，得了很好的成績。就是這四個民權，實在是經驗中的事實，不是假設來的理想，我們現在來採用，是很穩健的，並沒有甚麼危險。

至於說到政府權，從前都是由皇帝一個人壟斷，革命之後才分開成三個權，像美國獨立之後便實行三權分立，後來得了很好的成績，各國便都學美國的辦法。不過外國從前只有三權分立，我們現在爲甚麼要五權分立呢？其餘兩個權是從甚麼地方來的呢？這兩權是中國固有的東西。中國古時舉行考試和監察的獨立制度，也有很好的成績，像滿淸的御史，唐朝的諫議大夫，都是很好的監察制度。舉行這種制

they were very effective. The imperial censors or historiographers of the Manchu dynasty and the official advisers of the T'ang dynasty made a fine censoring system. The power of censorship includes the power to impeach, which other governments have but which is placed in the legislative body and is not a separate governmental power. The selection of real talent and ability through examinations has been characteristic of China for thousands of years. Modern foreign scholars who have studied Chinese institutions give high praise to China's old independent examination system, and there have been imitations of the system for the selection of able men in the West. Great Britain's civil service examinations are modeled after the old Chinese system, but only ordinary officials are examined. The British system does not yet possess the spirit of the independent examination system of old China. In Chinese political history, the three governmental powers—judicial, legislative, and executive—were vested in the emperor. The other powers of civil service examination and censorship were separate from the throne. The old autocratic government of China can also be said to have had three departments and so was very different from the autocratic gov-

度的大權，就是監察權，監察權就是彈劾權。外國現在也有這種權，不過把他放在立法機關之中，不能夠獨立成一種治權罷了。至於歷代舉行考試，拔取眞才，更是中國幾千年的特色。外國學者近來考察中國的制度，便極贊美中國考試的獨立制度，也有倣效中國的考試制度去拔取眞才。像英國近來舉行文官考試，便是說從中國倣效過去的。不過英國的考試制度，只考試普通文官，還沒有達到中國考試權之獨立的眞精神。所以就中國政府權的情形講，只有司法、立法、行政三個權是由皇帝拿在掌握之中，其餘監察和考試權還是獨立的，就是中國的專制政府從前也可以說是三權分立的，和外國從前的專制政府，便大不相同。從前外國在專制政府的時候，無論是甚麼權，都是由皇帝一個人龔斷。中國在專制政府的時候，關於考試權和監察權，皇帝還沒有龔斷。所以分開政府的大權，便可以說外國是三權分立，中國

ernments of the West in which all power was monopolized by the king or emperor himself. During the period of autocratic government in China, the emperor still did not have sole authority over the power of examination and censorship. So China in a way had three coordinate departments of government, just as the modern democracies of the West have their three departments, with this difference—the Chinese government has exercised the powers of autocracy, censorship, and civil examination for many thousands of years, while Western governments have exercised legislative, judicial, and executive powers for only a little over a century. However, the three governmental powers in the West have been imperfectly applied and the three coordinate powers of ancient China led to many abuses. If we now want to combine the best from China and the best from other countries and guard against all kinds of abuse in the future, we must take the three Western governmental powers—the executive, legislative, and judicial; add to them the old Chinese powers of examination and censorship and make a finished wall, a quintuple-power government. Such a government will be the most complete and the finest in the world, and a state with such a government

140

也是三權分立，中國從前實行君權，考試權和監察權的分立，有了幾千年。外國實行立法權、司法權和行政權的分立，有了一百多年，不過外國近來實行這種三權分立，還是不大完全，中國從前實行那種三權分立，更是有很大的流弊。我們現在要集合中外的精華，防止一切的流弊，便要採用外國的行政權、立法權、司法權，加入中國的考試權，和監察權，連成一個很好的完壁，造成一個五權分立的政府。像這樣的政府，才是世界上最完全最良善的政府。國家有了這樣的純良政府，才可以做到民有民治、民享的國家。

will indeed be of the people, by the people, and for the people.

Each of these four popular powers and five governmental. powers has its own focus and function; we must separate them clearly and not confuse them.

From the standpoint of function, the governmental powers are mechanical powers. In order to make this large machinery, which can develop tremendous horse power, function most effectively, we make it work in five directions. The popular powers are the powers of control which the people exercise directly over this high-powered machinery. The four powers of the people, we may say, are four controls which the people manipulate in order to make the machinery move and stop. The government works for the people and its five powers are five forms of work or five directions of work. The people control the government and their four powers are four methods of control. Only as the government is given such power and the opportunity to work in these different directions can it manifest great dignity and authority and become an all-powerful government. Only as the people are given great power and the various checks upon the government will they not be afraid

我們在政權一方面，主張四權，在治權一方面，主張五權。這四權和五權，各有各的統屬，各有各的作用，要分別清楚，不可紊亂。

殊不知道五權是屬於政府的權，就他的作用說，就是機器權。一個極大的機器，發生了極大的馬力，要這個機器所做的工夫，很有成績，便要把他分成五個做工的門徑。民權就是人民用來直接管理這架大馬力的機器之權，所以四個民權，就可以說是機器上的四個節制。有了這四個節制，便可以管理那架機器的動靜。政府替人民做事，要有五個權，就是要有五種工作，要分成五個門徑去做工。人民管理政府的動靜，要有四個權就是要有四個節制，要分成四方面來管理政府。政府有了這樣的能力，有了這些做工的門徑，才可以發出無限的威力，才是萬能政府。人民有了這樣大的權力，有了這樣多的節制，便不怕政府到了萬能，沒

141

of the government becoming all-powerful and uncontrollable. The people can then at any time command the government to move or to stop. The prestige of the government will grow and the power of the people will increase. With such an administrative power on the part of the government and such political power on the part of the people, we will be able to realize the ideal of the American scholar—an all-powerful government seeking the welfare of the people—and to blaze the way for the building of a new world.

有力量來管理。政府的一動一靜，人民隨時都是可以指揮的。像有這種情形，政府的威力便可以發展，人民的權力也可以擴充。有了這種政權和治權，才可以達到美國學者的目的，造成萬能政府，爲人民謀幸福。中國能够實行這種政權和治權，便可以破天荒在地球上造成一個新世界。

142